"YOU CAN TELL JUST BY LOOKING"

"YOU CAN TELL JUST BY LOOKING"

And 20 Other
Myths about LGBT Life and People

Michael Bronski

Ann Pellegrini

Michael Amico

BEACON PRESS
BOSTON

BEACON PRESS
25 Beacon Street
Boston, Massachusetts 02108-2892
www.beacon.org

Beacon Press books
are published under the auspices of
the Unitarian Universalist Association of Congregations.

16 15 14 13   8 7 6 5 4 3 2 1

This book is printed on acid-free paper that meets the uncoated paper
ANSI/NISO specifications for permanence as revised in 1992.

Composition by Wilsted & Taylor Publishing Services

Library of Congress Cataloging-in-Publication Data
Bronski, Michael.
"You can tell just by looking" : and 20 other myths about LGBT life and people /
Michael Bronski, Ann Pellegrini, Michael Amico.
    pages cm
Includes bibliographical references and index.
ISBN 978-0-8070-4245-8 (pbk.) —ISBN 978-0-8070-4246-5 (ebook)
1. Lesbians—United States. 2. Gays—United States. 3. Bisexuals—United States.
4. Transgender people—United States—History. 5. Gay liberation movement—
United States I. Pellegrini, Ann. II. Amico, Michael. III. Title.
HQ75.5.B7596 2013
306.76'6—dc23   2013023146

CONTENTS

Part 4: It's Just a Phase

PART 5: Struggling in the World

INTRODUCTION

In the 1890s, Lord Alfred Douglas famously described same-sex attraction as "the love that dare not speak its name." Since that time there has been a whole lot of talking. By the early 1970s, homosexuality had become, as many quipped, the love that won't shut up. American public life—the context for this book—is filled with claims and counterclaims about the nature and naturalness of homosexuality, the morality of same-sex marriage, and, increasingly, whether transgenderism is a disorder or just one gender identity among others. Acrimonious debates over these questions take place in arenas as diverse as pop culture, professional sports, and legislative politics.

In one of the most talked-about moments of the 2011 Grammy Awards, pop diva Lady Gaga bursts out of a shimmering, translucent egg to the propulsive beat of her LGBT anthem, "Born This Way." Later that year, she establishes the Born This Way Foundation to improve the lives and safety of LGBT youth. A lot of LGBT people dance to Gaga's beat; they deeply feel they were born attracted to the same sex or with a gender different from what others assigned to them, and embrace that identity and experience. Other LGBT people do not believe that, and with just as much Gagalike conviction claim they have chosen to be LGBT.

In September 2012, Brendon Ayanbadejo, a linebacker for the NFL's Baltimore Ravens, attracts the ire of a Democratic legislator in the Maryland General Assembly, Emmett C. Burns Jr. Ayanbadejo's offense? He has become a very public advocate for same-sex marriage. Another football player, Minnesota Vikings punter Chris Kluwe, gets in on the act, writing a colorful open letter to Burns. In it, Kluwe offers his support to Ayanbadejo and for same-sex marriage—and schools Burns on the meaning of free speech. Still, all is not homo-cosy in the hypermasculine world of professional sports. Just a week after the dust-up between Ayanbadejo and Burns, Toronto Blue Jays shortstop Yunel Escobar sports black eye tape during a game with an antigay slur written on it in Spanish. He is suspended for three games.

In June 2013, the Supreme Court rules on two important marriage-equality cases. Holding that the third section of the 1996 Defense of Marriage Act (DOMA) is unconstitutional, the Court now allows legally married same-sex couples access to all federal benefits available to heterosexual married couples, including a multitude of tax and Social Security benefits. The decision also eases the immigration process for binational couples. (In a striking coincidence, the DOMA decision is handed down ten years to the day that the Supreme Court, in *Lawrence v. Texas*, overturned laws criminalizing consensual homosexual sex.) In the second highly watched case, the Court rules on Proposition 8, which defined marriage in California as only between a man and a woman, and reversed a ruling allowing marriage equality. Side-stepping the substance of the case—the constitutionality of state bans on same-sex marriage—the Court holds that the groups bringing suit to defend Proposition 8 do not have the legal standing to do so. This narrow decision leaves in place a lower court ruling overturning Proposition 8 and opens the way to same-sex marriages in California again. The decision does not affect marriage equality in other states because the regulation of marriage is traditionally left to the states. As a result, marriage equality for same-sex couples remains a state-by-state proposition, with only thirteen states and the District of Columbia currently permitting same-sex couples to marry.

In July 2013, the Employment Non-Discrimination Act, which would bar most public and private employers from discriminating against potential or current employees on the basis of sexual orientation and gender identity, finally makes it out of a Senate committee for a full vote by the Senate. As this book goes to press, a vote by the full Senate has not yet been scheduled, though Senate Majority Leader Harry Reid has confirmed his interest in doing so soon. Even if the bill succeeds in the Senate, however, it has no chance of passage in the Republican-controlled House of Representatives. Supporters have been trying to pass a version of this law since 1974. In an end run around earlier congressional inaction, the federally appointed Equal Employment Opportunity Commission had already ruled, in April 2012, that Title VII of the 1964 Civil Rights Act, which prohibits discrimination on the basis of sex, applies to gender identity as well. In practice, this means that government agencies can no longer discriminate against transgender employees or applicants because of their gender identity. The ruling does not apply to employees of private companies.

As the preceding examples show, we are in the midst of simultaneous, rapid legal and social changes, even as pernicious stereotypes and outright inequality persist.

This book is an attempt to help readers clear through the thicket of these and many other hot-button issues. We want to dispel harmful, often hostile, myths, stereotypes, and false assumptions about LGBT people. But we also want to explain what myths do, how they work and move in the world, and why the myths in this book remain so compelling even when they are shown to be false. How and why do gut feelings solidify into hard-and-fast facts about the world? How has society allowed some myths that are manifestly untrue to flourish and circulate as fact?

The challenge of this book is about more than beating back anti-LGBT lies. We also scrutinize the claims that LGBT people make about themselves. What myths do they believe about their own lives and culture, and why?

Before we discuss specific myths, we need to give some brief background about LGBT people and their culture. A large and still growing body of scholarship shows that the meanings of same-sex desire and gender variation are culturally and historically particular. It's not just that the names "lesbian," "gay," "bisexual," and "transgender" are relatively new additions to the English language; so are the identities they name.

Hungarian social reformer Karl-Maria Kertbeny coined the word "homosexual" in 1868, using it publicly in a political pamphlet the following year to promote homosexual emancipation. Kertbeny's acts of classification and naming were done in the service of homosexual rights. But his model of innate sexual desires opened the door for early sexologists, women and men who attempted to look at sex and human nature in a scientific manner, to identify "homosexuality" as a type of sexual abnormality and pathologize "gender deviancy" as one of its manifestations.

Categories and labels are not static. From the early decades of the twentieth century forward, LGBT people have contested these negative judgments and fought to wrest control over their own names and identities. In so doing, they have been able to secure increased visibility and acknowledgment in culture and society. These important efforts to reclaim and revalue terms once used to disparage them have also reinforced the idea that sexual identity marks the definitive truth about a person and provoked increasing debates about this "truth."

In June 2012, CNN anchor Anderson Cooper disclosed he was gay, to the surprise of some and the "about time" response of others. Cooper, for his part, was walking a tightrope, trying to destigmatize gayness (his own and others') while simultaneously preserving the aura of neutrality and objectivity of someone who reports the news, rather than makes it. But is a homosexual identity ever a neutral standpoint?

All gender and sexual identities are creative fictions of a sort. Nevertheless, individuals whose sexual desires and gender expression conform to the norm are rarely asked to explain when or how they first knew they were straight, or why they believe they're really a woman. In contrast, people who deviate, or who are seen as deviating, from sexual and gender norms are commonly required to explain and justify their very existence. Similar burdens fall on people and communities who are racially and religiously different from dominant norms. Importantly, then, the moral weight and real-world impact of myths do differ depending on who is doing the talking.

The stories LGBT people tell about themselves often represent an attempt to explain and defend their existence in the face of legalized discrimination, social marginalization, and even outright violence. The idea that "gay people are just like straight people" (a concept that runs through so many of the myths discussed in this book) contains an obvious kernel of truth; all people share some basic similarities. But it obscures the fact that specific everyday realities and social structures have shaped the lives of LGBT people very differently than those of heterosexuals. It also sidesteps how the meaning and value of sexuality differ from person to person, gay and straight, and often even across an individual's lifetime. Many heterosexual people are not like "everyone else" either. Dismantling myths about LGBT life and people also involves unpacking myths about heterosexuals and the very idea of sexuality.

One of the functions of myths is to fill in gaps in knowledge between yourself and others, between us and them. Myths help to police the boundaries between same and different, known and unknown, setting up some differences (whiteness, heterosexuality, Christianity, able-bodiedness) as the very measure of what it is to be normal, natural, and properly human. But all of us also differ from the ideal selves we think we have to be. Confusion and fear about these differences can lead to an inability to see facts that do not fit a particular person's, or entire community's, self-understandings— including our own.

A desire for short, quick answers to complicated questions about how to live with differences and unknowns about people has generated myths on both "pro-LGBT" and "anti-LGBT" sides. We are all used to hearing rhetoric such as "Sexual abuse causes homosexuality" or "Gay rights infringe on religious liberty" from people who see the rising public presence of LGBT people as detrimental to society. We are also used to hearing LGBT people and their allies counter with their own inflated and factually unsupported claims, such as "Hate crime laws prevent violence against LGBT people" and "About 10 percent of people are gay or lesbian."

The three authors of this book—all of whom share an unwavering commitment to expanding equality and freedom for LGBT people—are deeply sympathetic to the complex reasons behind such ostensibly pro-LGBT myths. We are aware that in criticizing certain myths held by LGBT people, we risk accusations that this book is "bad" for LGBT people because we are publicly airing disagreements within this community. First, a myth is no less a myth if it is marshaled for "good" purposes than for "bad" ones. Second, we think that social progress and meaningful freedom for LGBT people are best advanced by creating the space not just for queer differences from the mainstream, but also for differences within the LGBT community.

The idea that "LGBT" is a single, clearly defined cultural entity is itself a myth. Being "gay," being "lesbian," being "bisexual," and being "transgender" are all distinct experiences. While there are some similarities—for example, all LGBT people know what it feels like to be outsiders—these groups are often separated by more than what joins them together. Even the experience of being "othered" and discriminated against differs across L, G, B, and T, and within each of these identity categories, too. LGB people are not always welcoming of transgender people. Sexism has historically impeded alliances between gay men and lesbians. Moreover, race, religion, class, and national origins profoundly affect how gender identity and sexual desire are experienced. They also shape which bodies are singled out for hostile attention and which, for protection.

Gay men and lesbians began organizing in political action groups in the 1950s. By the mid-1970s, bisexual women and men, who had worked in these movements, wanted recognition of their presence, and they fought to add the "B" to the "L" and "G." In the mid-1990s, transgender people also began to organize in national groups. Since they shared aspects of discrimination with lesbian, gay, and bisexual people because of the ways gender is intertwined with sexuality, "LGBT" became one coalition. This occurred even though many of the concerns and needs of transgender people were importantly different from those of LGB people. Today, we say LGBT, or often LGBTQI (adding "queer" and "intersex"), as though this mash-up were a politically obvious historical given. But it is important to remember that this acronym emerged slowly, and often through intense fighting, as some gay and lesbian people resisted adding B and T. In the end, however, each of these groups understood that they were stronger banding together around certain issues, as any coalition would be, than fighting alone.

In the name of promoting LGBT-positive positions, advocates may unintentionally promote restrictive ideas about what it means to be a "real" LGBT person. Community does not have to mean unity at all costs. What about all those LGBT people who do not think they are the same as "everyone else," including other LGBT people, and who have organized their lives and built diverse cultures and communities around their deeply felt differences? Aren't they LGBT, too? Beyond the no more than 5 percent of people who actually identify as L, G, or B in the United States, what about the many more who nonetheless act homosexually or have homosexual desires at some point in their lives? And beyond the approximately o.3 percent of people in the United States who identify as transgender, what about the many more who feel some disconnect between their gender presentation and their "male" or "female" body? This book makes room for dissenting positions and experiences that already exist in the world, but too often get left out of both anti- and pro-LGBT myths.

In some ways, this is a "how to" book for people who are arguing in the public arena about issues of LGBT life and rights. We provide readers with the concrete information, historical facts, and arguments they need to counter any of these myths in conversation or political discussions.

Undercutting the inaccuracy and power of a myth is not simply about correcting misinformation. One of our goals is to grapple with the complexities of what it means to be LGBT in the broadest social, emotional, psychological, political, cultural, and personal sense. That is why debunking each of the myths in this book means placing them in as wide and inclusive a context as possible, including how they relate to LGBT as well as straight people. In this regard, there may be more uncomfortable similarities than differences between how pro-LGBT myths and anti-LGBT myths work in the broader culture.

Myths are fueled by ambiguities and uncertainties around fundamental, yet complex, human realities that affect how we live in the world. Gender and sexuality are not reducible to the birds and the bees, nor to biological patterns and responses. Gender and sexuality are full of ambivalences and instabilities that pose more questions and possibilities than the binary categories male or female, straight or gay allow. That's why people get so upset by them, or are fascinated, even obsessed, by them.

There is no pure human sexuality or gender outside of the world that gives it meaning and purpose. For each myth, we discuss how and why it came into being and explain why its misinformation continues to be appealing to people. Arguably, anxieties over gender and sexuality condense much larger anxieties about what it means to have a body and be dependent on other bodies—on other people—for our very survival.

One of the reasons straight people have so many questions about LGBT people is that they lack accurate knowledge and understanding of their own sexuality. The questions they ask about LGBT people are often the unasked questions, fears, and wishes about their own sexuality and gender. Despite the prevalence of sex in US media and consumer culture, we still live in a culture that has a difficult time forthrightly discussing sexual issues. Myths are a way for these lurking anxieties and questions to be raised, discussed, and wishfully resolved.

Over the course of this book, readers will be taken through an encyclopedic range of materials. In this way, the book functions as a crash course in ideas and literature about LGBT life. We will be drawing on court cases, scientific and sociological studies, statistical analyses, histories, literary texts, and popular culture. Readers can approach the twenty-one myths by following the loose topical clusters, or they can go off-grid and chart their own paths. Either approach will shed light on the domino effect of misunderstandings impeding LGBT people and lives. Although each myth works as a stand-alone essay, cumulatively we want to show some common features in how myths function culturally and personally, the shared assumptions and shared anxieties they draw upon and reproduce.

These common features will also reveal some surprising and discomforting similarities between LGBT people and "everyone else." The dichotomy pro-LGBT versus anti-LGBT does not accurately reflect the way people's shared anxieties and assumptions about sexuality and gender are embedded in myths. Straight people are not the only ones who debate "How stable are sexual or gender identities?" and "When does a child become sexual?" and "How does parenting shape gender roles?" Nor are LGBT people the only ones who ever wonder "Am I normal?" and "Is it okay to desire this?"

Simply dispelling myths does not mean we will emerge with a clearer understanding of who LGBT people "truly" are, what their lives are "really" like, or what gender and sexuality essentially "are." To do so would turn this book into its own myth-machine. If anything, the reader's understandings of this material will be challenged and made more complex. Myths about LGBT people are so numerous that many readers may have specific ones they want to read about, but that are not included here. We do not claim to be exhaustive; nor could we be. We focus here on what we believe to be the most persistent and pernicious contemporary myths about LGBT people. The kinds of questions we raise will give readers a toolkit that they can then bring to bear in answering other myths not discussed in this book.

One major purpose of this book is to highlight the costs of staking good feelings, smooth relations, equality, and acceptance on simplistic understandings and myths. Here are five ways to classify myths and the social compromises they enforce in the world:

(1) Myths uphold existing social rules and expectations. Political and religious rhetoric repeatedly hammer home the mythological connections between homosexuality, gender deviancy, and all that is bad in the world. By focusing on the social conditions through which these myths operate, we question who determines what is and is not "true" or "safe" about homosexuality and gender nonconformity, why this is so, and whom the myth benefits.

(2) Myths erase the complications and differences of everyday lives. It is imperative to remember that while identity is necessary for political movements, there is no single LGBT, or straight, experience. How we talk about inclusion must honor rather than erase differences. Not every myth in this book applies equally to L, G, B, and T people; some focus on the connection between them, and many myths focus almost entirely on one or another letter of this alliance. This approach reflects our interest in tracking how individual experience and identity vary along the lines of gender, class, race, and religion. We do this to better understand sexuality and gender as they are lived and continually reinvented.

(3) Myths make uncomfortable questions somebody else's problem. Often, people who see themselves as the majority will focus on those who are not the norm, such as homosexuals or transgender people, to avoid larger social and cultural issues that make them uncomfortable. This book thus offers a minisurvey of Western culture's racism, prejudice toward women, and exclusion of religious minorities, showing how debates over sexuality and gender often become placeholders—hot seats—for anxieties about difference.

(4) Myths keep secrets. In a kind of bait and switch, many myths work to take attention away from their proponents by associating their own hang-ups with another group. These other groups come to stand for what is threatening and, perhaps, threateningly liberating, for society. The belief that, because you are not LGBT,

these myths have nothing to do with you is itself a myth. Same-sex attraction, or sexual curiosity, and gender ambiguity run through daily encounters, even between people who are not LGBT. None of us sees the world in a completely straight way, no matter what we may tell ourselves.

(5) Myths inhibit logical discussion. A myth's persuasiveness does not depend on its coherence or rationality. A myth works because it taps into preconceived notions of what is good or bad, just or unjust, pleasurable or disgusting. In this sense, a myth appeals to gut-level, emotionally laden understandings of the world. The desires a myth appeals to—such as the desire to feel safe or normal—can trump inconvenient, contradictory facts. Myths thrive even in the face of new knowledge, because they are designed to answer to the open-ended quality of continued confusion. As such, they cannot explain away underlying anxieties; they actually feed on them.

Myths help negotiate the messiness of personal and cultural histories that shape how we live and understand our lives. In this way, all myths express some kind of truth. Foregrounding their inconsistencies so that we can think about them openly and honestly does not make them any less complicated, nor does this have to lead to further division between people. An old progressive-movement axiom holds that it's only disagreement within movements, and the discussion that results, that move them forward.

There are no easy, and often no definitive, answers for enacting change in the world. The bottom line is that being gay or lesbian or bisexual or transgender is part of being human, and simply being human is very complicated. We want all readers, LGBT and straight, to engage, grapple with, and debate the issues in this book. Moreover, because myths are a central means for how LGBT people understand themselves as sexual beings, we want people in the LGBT community to question their own beliefs and why they hold them. Individuals, like cultures, can hold conflicting understandings of sexuality and gender. Admitting the inconsistencies of our own selves, rather than insisting on quick and easy answers, can generate new and unheard of possibilities for living in the world.

PART 1

LIVING IN THE WORLD

MYTH 1

YOU CAN TELL WHO'S GAY JUST BY LOOKING

You can certainly tell something just by looking, but what? In American slang, the word "gaydar" is commonly used to describe a special skill gay people possess, the ability to know at a glance whether someone else is gay or lesbian. In theory, gaydar decodes factors such as clothing, body language, facial expression, pitch of voice, and overall attitude.

Gay men and lesbians often discuss gaydar very tongue in cheek, as if it's a homosexual superpower of detection. But gaydar is more than a joke. It raises serious questions. In a world in which most people are presumed to be straight, how do lesbians and gay men find one another? Gaydar is invaluable in helping gay men and lesbians figure out whom they can safely flirt with. Is this a bromance or a potential romance? Is this a date or are we just having drinks after work?

Gaydar is, quite simply, a skill that everybody—gay or straight—has: intuition. We all have developed skills at reading signs and cues to assess whether someone is interested in us romantically or sexually. But intuition is not hard facts. How much do we need to know about a person to make a snap judgment? What kind of knowledge are we talking about here?

The myth that you can tell just by looking is part of an impulse to categorize and sort the world. The belief that it is possible to see, or "get," someone's sexuality from visible bodily traits, or listen for it in the lilt of a male voice or the deep alto of a woman's, comes in part from the widely held view that sexuality, and maybe especially a marginalized sexuality, is evident in every facet of a person's being. When a gay man walks down the street, he does so like gay men do. When a lesbian laughs at a joke, she is laughing like lesbians do. The individual is seen as inseparable from the group identity. And, if a gay person commits a crime, there is a presumption that it is connected to that individual's gayness, and that all gay people may want to do this too. In contrast, crimes committed by people who are seen as "mainstream" are never understood to be caused by their belonging to a specific group. When was the last time an editorial argued that Wall Street fraud revealed the potential criminality or untrustworthiness of all white men? If you belong to the dominant group, you get to be an individual. You are not representative of an entire group.

We commonly sort out people by sexuality, race, sex, religion— "just by looking." We are also frequently inaccurate. None of these identities is as readily detectable as we think. Accurate or not, however, this sorting affects our conscious and unconscious behavior toward people. No matter who we are, we might act differently around a white person (or a person we think is white) than a black person (or a person we think is black). This is also true for someone we identify as a woman rather than a man. Our behavior may also change around someone whose religious identity is visible to us by a yarmulke, turban, veil, or cross. At its worst, for many heterosexuals, the belief that you can tell who's gay just by looking rests on the belief that gay people will somehow stand out from the crowd because they can never really be part of the crowd.

Gaydar may be useful for lesbian and gay flirting, but there is a history of heterosexual gaydar, too. And it isn't pretty. Gay people are now allowed to serve openly in the armed forces, but in World War II psychiatrists developed their own version of gaydar to catch them if they attempted to enlist. These doctors assessed whether men and women fit a psychologically based homosexual type. They conducted interviews and physical exams to see if a recruit expressed a sense of superiority or fear because both were associated with homosexuality. They looked for signs of traditional masculinity or effeminacy in men's bodies, mannerisms, emotional makeup, and interests.[1] They used similar calculations for women who enlisted. But this was more complicated since volunteering for military service already placed women into a traditionally nonfeminine role. Of the sixteen million men who enlisted, only about ten thousand were rejected after being identified as homosexual.[2] This was far, far fewer than the number of those who were actually homosexual or who would have homosexual relations during their time in the military.

Was the medical gaydar not working? In numerous cases the doctors let lesbians or gay men join because the military needed troops. But the larger reality was that doctors weren't seeing everything. Their measures were simply not reflective of how people displayed, never mind lived, their sexuality. Worse, the gender stereotypes these tests used led to discrimination and abuse. Some lesbians and gay men could easily "pass" to be accepted, but some could never pass—then or now—even if they wanted to.

The gender stereotypes of homosexuality were connected to then-contemporary explanations of homosexuality. In 1947, psychoanalyst Clara Thompson wrote that lesbianism was caused by improper parental role models and excess leisure time during childhood. Lesbian adults manifested these root causes in later life via gender nonconformity, or mannishness, and aimless lounging about. Thompson believed a trained specialist could spot lesbianism by looking for these signs. Psychiatrists also linked particular professions to these gender stereotypes. People, straight and gay, still equate florist with gay man and UPS driver with lesbian.

These gender stereotypes also shape ideas for straight people about how they are not supposed to look. Many heterosexuals are very careful not to exhibit "gay" looks or behavior. Straight men who go out to dinner together, sometimes referred to as a man date, may choose a restaurant that does not look or feel romantic.

Despite the negative effects of the World War II psychiatrists, not all gender role stereotypes are detrimental. Depending on who is looking, these stereotypes can help gay people find partners and even form communities. For example, by the 1930s, lesbians had created butch, femme, and kiki (indicating women who were neither butch nor femme) gender roles to indicate the kind of sexual partner they desired. Butch/femme borrowed aspects of male/female gender differences, but asserted them in a very different sexual and political context.

Gay men's and lesbians' uses of coded signs and stereotypes to spot others were not necessarily a fun game, but vitally necessary for safety. Until 2003, when the Supreme Court issued its ruling in *Lawrence v. Texas*, same-sex sexual activity was illegal in many states. Gay men, for example, developed a system of codes so they could identify one another without being as easily identifiable to the law. They used types of dress, hairstyles, affectation, and gesture to communicate their identity. They might also use phrases with particular vocal stresses to convey interest. There were several meanings to the phrases "Have a light?" or "Nice day." In the first half of the twentieth century, when gay men needed to form communities in order to find sexual partners, they used these codes to meet in bars and restaurants; paradoxically, homosexual privacy could be had only in public.[3] Often the desire for this prohibited socializing, along with the complexity of these secret signs, gave gay male life an added erotic charge.

The history of how lesbian and gay men communicated desire between one another tells us that looking is only one aspect of telling. Messages between people make sense only in a larger context and in relation to others. What there is to tell depends on what you're looking for: immediate sexual pleasure, flirtation, conversation, or something else. People aren't always looking for the same thing. They may not even know what they're looking for. Desire and attraction are not straightforward or logical. They are filled with ambivalence, ambiguity, and mystery.

Eyes—how we look—communicate many things. A steadily held

gaze can be a form of sensual touch and invitation. Looking can also be a form of aggression, in the sense of staring someone down. Experts on body language say that we hold our gaze with people we like or we want to like us.[4] Eye contact is one of the most intimate forms of communication because a look or gaze can only be held between two people at a time. If someone does not meet and return our gaze, we assume that person is not interested. A long, lingering look between two people is often quickly sexualized. While we don't really know what other people are thinking, our imagination fills out their thoughts, making our desirous conjectures very real. We then wonder, "Will the other person imagine along with me?" And if or when this look becomes a stare, we worry, "Will the other person beat me up?" Looking brings to the surface many possibilities, some good, some dangerous.

Recent experiments on the science of gaydar have explored how we process our impressions, and even our desire. Mainstream media have frequently exaggerated the modest, preliminary conclusions of many of these studies and proclaimed, "Yes, gaydar is real!" As we've seen, there is something very real about it. We also must place all such claims about gaydar in context. These studies help us understand how much more complicated and unknowable that context might be.

Nicholas Rule, an openly gay psychologist, has taken the lead on exploring the science of gaydar. He has conducted experiments that ask participants to determine whether a person is gay or straight based on how that person appears in a photograph. The photos are taken from profiles of people who self-identified as gay, lesbian, or straight on dating and hookup sites. Participants look at these photos out of their original context. They have no clue whether a particular photo was taken from a gay, lesbian, or straight site. Fascinatingly, Rule's studies show that the accuracy rate in picking out lesbians and gay men from straight men and women is, on average, 64 percent. This result is "significantly better," he explains, than the 50 percent that chance guessing would yield. Most important, this accuracy rate holds steady even when a participant views only a subject's eyes, excluding eyebrows and even wrinkles, or just the mouth. The race or gender of the participants who were trying to determine the subjects' sexual identity, or that of the subjects themselves, had no effect on the accuracy rate. Neither did racial stereotypes of, for example, Asian men as effeminate and, thus, gay, or of black men as masculine and, thus, straight.

The results of Rule's experiments become even more suggestive when you consider that the accuracy rate has remained the same when study participants view the images, including just the eyes or mouth, at millisecond speeds. We don't know what participants "saw" in a face or eyes or a mouth. All that these studies prove is that participants often connected something in these images with the photographic subjects' self-identified sexuality.

How can we explain these results? Could self-identifying as gay or straight affect how a person's eyes or mouth appear? Is that just magical thinking? Does the legibility of sexual identity in these studies have something to do with the subject "wanting" to be read as one of three supposedly distinct identities: lesbian, gay, or straight? Importantly, people who identified as bisexual were not accurately judged at levels higher than chance.

We all decipher desire—whether cruising in a bar, attending a work party, sitting in the bleachers at a ball game—according to certain rules. These rules vary with the situation and shape our actions and responses accordingly. Rules can take the form of signs that cue us in to what might be an appropriate response. But what happens when we do not have obvious cues or stereotypes to lean on? What are we supposed to do then? Can our very desire to know something about a person also function as a kind of constraint, or rule, that directs where and how we look? The fact that our imagination is at play here does not make gaydar any less accurate. Empathy works in a similar way. When we feel empathy for others, we often want them to know that we know how it feels to be in their shoes, because we've experienced something similar. Empathy allows people to infer or read emotion across cultures and groups. Of course, greater famil- iarity with a particular culture offers additional help. One of Rule's

studies shows that gay men are more consistently accurate in identifying homosexuality than straight men. Might desire and empathy
be working together?

We want to know more. We want to see more. This does not
mean we instinctively know what is behind a face. Nor does it mean
that the totality and complexity of each person's sexuality can be
seen with complete accuracy. Rather than thinking about a person's
sexuality as his or her essence, or even as a containable and, thus,
an easily identified and measurable part, we should think about
sexuality as a process. When two people, gay or straight, are looking at each other with desire across a room, maybe they are asking
themselves what they like about each other and who they really are.

If we think about sexuality in this way—as a form of unspoken
communication, as an ongoing question rather than an answer—it
may open up an intriguing possibility for all the manifestations of
gaydar. At heart, maybe gaydar has nothing to do with seeing either
gayness or gayly, but seeing desire. Can a person indicate by look
and demeanor, even in a photograph, that he or she is approach-
able? Sexuality is a matrix of associations that paints a picture of
each of us. Looking creates an intimate world of human relations.
Can telling by looking, and the give and take between people, not
just communicate desire but actually instigate it? In some ways,
"You can tell just by looking" may be a very subversive idea. It opens
the door to new conversations about what we see, how we see, and
what it means to us. Gaydar is less about spotting (for good or ill)
gay people than it is about how we all communicate desire.

The hysteria surrounding homosexuality in our culture betrays
a deep-seated fear: gay people are not really different from other
people but rather too much like everyone else—and maybe everybody is a little bit gay, and a little bit straight. The myth that you can
tell just by looking reveals that sexuality and sexual desire do not so
readily sort themselves into the categories of gay or straight. When
you lock eyes with a person, whether or not you're attracted to each
other, you can make sense of the world you create together only by
leaving many preconceived ideas, beliefs, and identities behind.

MYTH 2

ABOUT 10 PERCENT OF PEOPLE ARE GAY OR LESBIAN

Just how many gay people are there? The most commonly cited statistic is that 10 percent of any population is gay, lesbian, or bisexual. This number is taken from what are commonly referred to as the Kinsey Reports. Alfred Kinsey was a zoologist and sexologist who, along with a team of researchers, published *Sexual Behavior in the Human Male*, in 1948, and *Sexual Behavior in the Human Female*, in 1953. He and his team conducted two-hour interviews with more than eleven thousand people: 5,300 men and 5,940 women, from early teens to ninety, although most were between college age and middle age. The interview pool represented a diverse population with respect to class and religion. The participants were almost all white, although Kinsey believed that his previous research on African Americans bore out his findings in the Kinsey Reports. The study's interviewees were asked about every possible combination of sexual behavior in which they had ever engaged: heterosexual, homosexual, masturbatory, voyeuristic, and even bestial. Interviewees were asked to detail sexual positions and fantasies, and whether they'd had sex before marriage or any extramarital affairs.

The 10 percent figure appears only once in relation to homosexuality in either report. Kinsey discovered that 10 percent of US males are "more or less exclusively homosexual" in their behavior for at least three years between the ages of sixteen and fifty-five. (During that time, 8 percent were, in fact, exclusively homosexual, and among women, 2–6 percent were "more or less" exclusively homosexual.) For Kinsey and his team, homosexuality occurring over a three-year period indicated that it was a significant feature of that person's sexual life. But the conclusion that 10 percent of the people in any given population are lesbian or gay is a serious misreading of Kinsey's work.

To compound matters, Kinsey consistently argued against identifying people as having homosexual or heterosexual identities. He was interested in what people did, not in how they self-identified.

Why do gay people, and LGBT organizations, continually cite this 10 percent figure, ignoring Kinsey's important cautions against conflating behaviors and identities? Gay people understandably want to feel that there are a lot of other people like them. But there is more to the history of how this number has been used. When Kinsey's first study was published, the 10 percent figure, out of literally thousands and thousands of statistics in the book, was reported and recycled in the initial, and scandalized, press coverage. The disproportionate attention given homosexuality, analysis of which had comprised less than a tenth of the first book, is due to the fact that, suddenly, straight America was confronted with evidence that, in their midst, there were so many more people engaging in homosexual behavior than they had thought or feared. The sensationalized reporting contributed to the book's huge sales and notoriety. It also lost Kinsey his government funding. Both *Sexual Behavior in the Human Male* and *Sexual Behavior in the Human Female* were best sellers, and together they have sold more than three-quarters of a million copies.

Before conducting his research, Kinsey suspected there was more homosexual behavior in the United States than anyone admitted. His progressive attitudes toward sexuality informed his desire to prove it. At the time of his studies, homosexual behavior was illegal in America. Kinsey hoped that by making an accurate assessment of the frequency of homosexual behavior, demonstrating that it was not isolated to a few individuals, his work would destigmatize homosexuality. He thought this might even lead to a change in laws.

The principal objective of Kinsey's research was to discover the most accurate way to measure all human sexual behavior. This raises an important question. While it is possible, within limits, to measure homosexual behavior, is it possible to scientifically study what it means to be "gay"? Or is "gay" a political and social identity? Or, rather, a moral question? Can it be all of these? Kinsey turned to a scientific study of people's sexual activity as a way to respond to, and potentially counter, American culture's intense moralizing around sex. As he and his team wrote in *Sexual Behavior in the Human Female*, because humans are so quick to categorize, we think that "[t]hings are either so, or they are not so. Sexual behavior is either normal or abnormal, socially acceptable or unacceptable, heterosexual or homosexual; and many persons do not want to believe that there are gradations in these matters from one to the other extreme."[1] This sounds very scientific; but if we, as a culture, admit to these gray areas, we may also stop thinking about sex in the context of black-and-white morality. Kinsey saw his objective science as a way of changing social views about sexuality and, with them, society itself. Returning to Kinsey's studies today may help us rethink the complexity of human sexuality.

In his research, Kinsey measured both behavior and arousal so he would have a more complete picture of human sexuality. These two measurements gave a complex account of an individual's sexual responses. He preferred to use the terms homosexual and heterosexual to describe sexual activities between persons, not the persons themselves. For Kinsey, the definition of homosexuality meant being sexual with, or aroused by, the same sex.

One of Kinsey's most important findings was that most people, in behavior and arousal, fell somewhere in between completely homosexual or heterosexual. Kinsey concluded that only about 4 percent of men and 1–3 percent of women are exclusively homosexual in their attractions and/or behavior throughout their lives; 50 percent are exclusively heterosexual; and 46–48 percent are sexually active with and/or aroused by both sexes. This means that, although few people act exclusively homosexually, almost half of all people do have a homosexual experience or are aroused by the idea of one. By demonstrating that there were as many people having homo sexual experiences as heterosexual ones, Kinsey's statistics normalized and de-moralized homosexuality. Moreover, because Kinsey's studies were considered more scientific and comprehensive than any previous such research, they had a sizable impact on popular thought at the time. Many of his findings do hold up today. The results of the most recent comprehensive study of human sexuality, *The National Survey of Sexual Health and Behavior* (2010), generally parallel Kinsey's findings regarding homosexual behavior. Contemporary researchers into sexuality still consider the Kinsey Reports as providing the most nuanced existing data about homosexuality because of their use of in-depth interviews.

Although Kinsey was not interested in what caused particular sexual desires, he was interested in how context and circumstance could affect how a person came to desire someone of the same sex. He thus examined how factors such as age, education, regional location, and religion helped shape expressions of homosexuality. He discovered that religion might affect family gender dynamics and that education in a single-sex college offered opportunities for same-sex sociality. Why people desired someone of the same sex was a different question.

Kinsey's data conclusively show that sexual preferences, behaviors, responses, and attractions can and often do vary across a person's lifetime and circumstances. Almost all of his statistics are qualified by the age of the subject. For example, he found that 37 percent of males he interviewed had, at some point between adolescence and old age, reached orgasm with another male. He also found that 50 percent of men who held off marrying until the age of thirty-five had engaged in sex with another man to orgasm.

The statistics for women were strikingly different. The occurrence of homosexual responses in females was half as much as that in males. Homosexual contact to orgasm was one-third as much. Finally, a much smaller percentage of women continued their homosexuality for as many years as the men did. Only half to a third as many females were exclusively homosexual. Gender shaped the patterns of sexual life in other ways, too. Kinsey concluded that two females were more likely to remain in a steady relationship than two men, hypothesizing that the display of affection between women was more socially acceptable. This conclusion, though, might as easily, or better, be explained by the fact that women are socialized to be in long-term committed relationships. Kinsey also concluded that men who had sex with men had many more sexual partners than did women who had sex with women, because sexual promiscuity was highly valorized among men. These conclusions, accurate or not, are still held to be true today. The reality is that cultural assumptions shape how people express themselves sexually. Long-standing stereotypes around sexuality—such as ideas about who is promiscuous and who is monogamously faithful—are largely organized around presumed differences between men and women.

Some people invoke statistics to show that homosexuality is relatively rare. Others crunch numbers to demonstrate that more gay people exist, and have always existed, than is commonly acknowledged. But Kinsey's data point to something far more radical. His findings show that very few people stably fit any one category. Sex and desire are complex. His findings hold implications for everyone, and that is why there continues to be so much resistance to his work. Many lesbians and gay men have not wanted to hear about individual sexual variance. They would rather, incorrectly, extrapolate the 10 percent number to all cultures and all periods in human history.

When so much of the present-day experience of gay and lesbian people tells them that they should not even exist, the desire to locate others like themselves in the past is understandable. Discovering that you and people like you have a history is a way to believe you have a future. All evidence points to the fact that people have experienced same-sex desire, and engaged in same-sex practices, across cultures and human history. What these practices and desires have meant and whether they have been praised or condemned have not been constant across time or place. This, too, is history, and it fits well with Kinsey's own interest in finding out what people do, what they think about what they do, and how this is understood in relation to the prevailing social rules. By shedding light on the rich array of human sexual practices and imaginations, Kinsey's research reveals different ways to be gay. It opens up different ways to consider what being gay means today as well as in the past.

Kinsey's studies have also come in for a lot of appropriate criticism. Social scientists, both in his day and in ours, have criticized the composition of his studies. People have argued that the research did not track the same people over an extended amount of time and that the sample was not nationally representative. Others note the study may have unintentionally selected for interviewees more willing to share homosexual histories, because talking to Kinsey's research teams was a rare chance to talk about "deviant" sex without being judged for it. Along this line, others argue that male prisoners were overrepresented in the sample, probably increasing the number of men reporting having had sex with other men. Kinsey also interviewed people who were already part of homosexual communities.

Culture and circumstance no doubt shaped Kinsey's studies in very particular ways. But these factors always shape and transform the expression of sexuality itself. We cannot understand sexuality outside of them. For example, many more-recent studies have discovered a far higher occurrence of homosexual contacts between women than did Kinsey. Often these rates exceed that of male same-sex sexual behavior. Does this reversal reflect changes in cultural attitudes? Does it reveal the particular power dynamics at play in the Kinsey studies, where women were almost always interviewed by male researchers? Any one interviewee or study participant can lie—whether in the face-to-face interviews used by Kinsey and his team or in the anonymous questionnaires used in more-recent surveys. People often lie about sex or bend the truth to others and even to themselves. Psychological motivation and sense of self are always difficult to assess. If Kinsey had focused only on arousal, feelings, and other psychological responses, then ascertaining sexuality might have been always just out of reach. But if he had focused only on behavior, then he might seriously underreport, because he found that many people continued to fantasize about a variety of sexual acts that they rarely—if ever—engaged in.

Kinsey took all of this into consideration in developing the Kinsey Scale as a measure of a person's sexuality. The scale is distinct from the majority of Kinsey's statistics. It simultaneously takes into account both feelings of arousal and actual behavior that did and did not end in orgasm. It was developed to show that more people behaved sexually in various ways than a focus on orgasm or a sexual act would reveal. Among other things, the scale helps us get a picture of the many gradations in sexual life, such as instances where individuals may be sexually aroused by members of the same sex but never act on these desires. The scale ranges from 0 to 6: 0 means exclusively heterosexual, and 6, exclusively homosexual; the wide variety of people who behaved and fantasized bisexually existed somewhere in between.

Each number along the scale measures the balance of homosexual and heterosexual behavior and/or arousal in any one person's sexual history. Someone who is a Kinsey 6, meaning exclusively homosexual, might never have acted on any same-sex desires. What makes this person a 6 is that he or she does not have any consciously avowed sexual feelings toward the "opposite sex." Or, a person may be a 2 because he or she has, in fact, had a few homosexual experiences but still feels an overwhelming amount of desire for the "opposite sex." As Kinsey and his team wrote, "It is only possible to determine how many persons belong, at any particular time, to each of the classifications on a heterosexual-homosexual scale."[2] In other words, the rating is a snapshot of a particular moment, and may or may not predict a person's later behavior or self-identifications as lesbian, gay, bisexual, or straight.

If all sexuality is ultimately individual, and always circumstantial, can we ever make any general claims about homosexuality and LGB people—other than, it's complicated? The problem is that, ever since the publication of the Kinsey Reports, both heterosexuals and homosexuals, and in particular gay and lesbian organizations, have tried to use Kinsey's numbers to prove one point or another. It would be more useful to stop using the statistics for political purposes and, instead, use them as a resource for understanding what it means to be gay or bisexual or heterosexual. Sometimes, as when arguing for gay rights, it may prove useful and necessary to quote statistics and speak of "homosexual" and "heterosexual" as precise terms that describe clearly defined identities and groups. But we should not confuse political necessity with exploring and reveling in the richness, complexity, and sometimes downright confusions of sexual desire.

Ultimately, the point should not be to crunch numbers or explain who is gay or not gay, but to think about how people experience, negotiate, and live their desires as they move through the world. This shifting experience of desire is not going to produce such poster-ready lines as, "One Out of Ten People is Gay." Understanding the wide variety of ways people live their desires will open more social space for all people—however they identify—to be a little more honest about what they do and what they want with one another.

MYTH 3

ALL TRANSGENDER PEOPLE HAVE SEX-REASSIGNMENT SURGERY

The subject of transgenderism has only recently been discussed in the mainstream media. Even people in the gay, lesbian, and bisexual communities do not fully understand the complexities of transgender experience. Transgender is a large category, and it is necessary to be cautious with generalizations. The term "transgender" is often used to refer to people who consciously resist the conventional associations among an inner sense of gender (gender identity), the public expression of gender (gender roles or appearances), and the gender assigned at birth (biological sex). One feature shared by many, if not all, transgender people is the experience of incongruence between their gender identity and biological sex.

Contrary to the myth, some, but not all, transgender people undergo sex-reassignment surgery. This is a medical procedure that alters a person's secondary and sometimes primary sexual characteristics—breasts, ability to grow facial hair, genitals—to help produce a match between gender identity and the outer appearance of gender. Changing gender appearance to conform to the desired gender is not just about what other people see. It is as much about affirming an inner sense of self. But sex-reassignment surgery is only one of many options open to transpeople today.

Many nontransgender people cannot imagine the experience of being in the "wrong" body, let alone continuing to live, and live happily, with a serious disconnect between gender identity and biological sex. They assume that all transgender people want to transition to the "opposite sex" and will necessarily, and gladly, undergo sex-reassignment surgery to achieve this goal. This misguided belief is due, in part, to the increasing visibility of transgender people. The more transgender issues are discussed, the more questions and opinions nontransgender people will have. But it is also due to the fact that advances in medical technologies have, in the past decades, facilitated changing physical sex characteristics. To nontransgender people, the surgery may seem extreme, but the desired goal is not. For them, the correspondence between inside and outside reaffirms the widely accepted idea that there are two, and only two, genders. But what about those many people, both transgender and nontransgender, for whom this model of two and only two does not fit?

Questioning your gender and even changing how you express your gender are very common occurrences. We all present—or "perform"—our gender in very different ways. Most of these expressions may fall, to varying degrees, within the traditional standard of a female and male gender system. However, some people's gender identity and presentation do not fit easily within these traditional roles. Some people resist prescribed gender roles simply because they do not fit into them. Others may resist these roles because they do not believe they are useful or even healthy.

In today's culture, transgender people have come to be defined only by their gender variance, which is often pathologized as deviance. As a result, they are seen as extreme in their gender presentation. But there is nothing stable, definite, or normal about anyone's gender.

Rather than referring to nontransgender people as normatively gendered, or just men and women, some people now use the word "cisgender" to refer to individuals whose inner gender identity, outer gender expression, and assigned gender at birth overlap and do so in ways that feel seamless and natural (*cis* is from the Latin for "on this side"). Cisgender is sometimes inaccurately used to describe anyone who is not trans-identified. Many nontransgender people also feel that there is a gap between their inner gender identity and how they present themselves and are received by others.

In other words, even nontransgender people have to work at "being" a woman or "being" a man. Think of all of the magazines that illustrate how to be the perfect woman or man: *Vogue*, *Men's Health*, *Today's Bride*, *GQ*. Can anyone live up to these ideals? Our culture's fascination with transgender people and their changing bodies might even represent a covert recognition of how much work it takes for anyone to be a woman or a man. Transgender people show everyone else the tremendous effort, and possibly the pleasure, of having or becoming any gender at all.

Just as there are many ways to be a woman or a man, there are many ways to be transgender. These have come about in conjunction with, and been enabled by, the many ways all people manipulate and perform their gender. All of these changes are functions of historical developments, advancing technologies, and generational differences. Feminist challenges to gender-role stereotypes are certainly part of the backstory as well, despite the ambivalence and outright hostility some feminists have expressed to transgender people, especially to male-to-female transsexuals.[1]

To look at the many ways transgender people live their lives today, we need to examine how transgender people lived in the past. This includes examining the language that they have used to describe their lives and how ideas about gender have changed over time. The phenomenon of transgenderism has long roots in history and in a wide variety of cultures, even though the terms we may use today have come into common usage only in the past century and continue to evolve.

In *Transgender Warriors: Making History from Joan of Arc to Ru-Paul*, Leslie Feinberg charts a long, complex, sometimes hidden, but often very public, history of people who boldly challenged the gender norms of their time. Joan of Arc famously donned soldiers' clothes to lead French troops against the British in the early fifteenth century. She was placed on trial for heresy, and some of the charges against her included the sin (as it was then defined in Roman Catholic canon law) of cross-dressing. She was convicted and burned at the stake. Christian Davies was born a woman and cross-dressed and fought in the 2nd North British Dragoons in the early eighteenth century. In the late eighteenth century, Charles-Geneviève-Louis-Auguste-André-Timothée d'Éon de Beaumont, usually called the Chevalier d'Éon, was a soldier and a spy for the French, who dressed as both a woman and a man and famously kept most of Europe guessing about his anatomical sex for his entire life. (It is from his name that we derive the word "eonism," an early medical term diagnosing male-to-female cross-dressing.) We also know that many women cross-dressed as soldiers during the American Civil War. There has also been a vibrant history of "passing women"—that is, women who passed as men—throughout European and American history, and outside of soldiering. Mary Fields, often called Stagecoach Mary, was born a woman and a slave. In 1895, at the age of 60, she was hired as a man by the US postal service because of her speed in harnessing horses and driving a stagecoach.

In the 1930s, when medical technology made it possible to perform sex-reassignment surgery, some women and men began to physically change their sex. In the late 1940s, Laura Maud Dillon underwent surgery and became Lawrence Michael Dillon. In 1951, Robert Cowell, a British World War II fighter pilot, underwent surgery and became Roberta Cowell. These cases received some public attention; Cowell wrote a book about her life in 1954. But in 1952 the world became acutely aware of the medical possibilities of what was now being termed transsexualism when former US Army member George Jorgensen underwent surgery and became the glamorous Christine Jorgensen. Within weeks, Jorgensen became the most famous transsexual in the world and an object of enormous media interest and speculation. The idea of a "sex change" operation fascinated the world—and not only because it opened new possibilities of how we could understand gender and sex.

After World War II, there was an enormous interest in the possibilities of science, which could now not only send rockets into space, and ultimately put a man on the moon, but build the hugely destructive atomic bomb and change a person's sex. In the popular imagination, the terrifying atomic bomb was closely connected to gender and sexuality. Marilyn Monroe and other platinum-haired female Hollywood stars were called "blonde bombshells." Even the new two-piece bathing suit for women was called the bikini, after Bikini Atoll, where the first atomic bomb was tested in 1946. During this period, language used to describe gender-variant people also changed. Those who dressed in the clothing of the "opposite sex" were often called cross-dressers or transvestites (*trans* is from the Latin for "across," and *vestite* means "to dress"). The new surgery gave us the word "transsexual."

Over the decades, wide-ranging cultural changes—from the traditional roles women and men were able to play in society to changing social mores about appropriate dress and grooming—made a radical impact on American ideas about gender. For example, by the mid-1970s pantsuits on women were perfectly acceptable, and men could wear their hair long and don colorful clothing and jewelry. Things were changing for transgender people as well. Advances in hormone treatments in the 1970s allowed people to take on some secondary sex characteristics of another sex, such as growing facial hair, changing their voice, and sculpting musculature and body shape. Transpeople were now able to take on the physical appearance of another sex without having a full sex-reassignment surgery.

By the 1990s, there was a new tolerance, although still a great amount of fear and discrimination, regarding the various ways people enacted gender. Today, terms such as transsexual and even transvestite are used less and less. (The one exception is the use of transvestite, or cross-dresser, to describe women and men who do this as professional entertainers.) The experience of being transgender is also very different today from what it was two decades ago, and certainly from before that. Many more people now identify as transgender and for a wider range of reasons. Sometimes, rather than changing their bodies through surgery or hormones, this may mean changing a gender identification from male or female to the other sex, and using sex-appropriate pronouns to reinforce that identity. Still, many transpeople are acutely aware of the limits of a binary gender system and do not feel comfortable conforming to traditional gender norms.

There are also people who actively protest gender norms. They may go out of their way to flaunt conventions, perhaps wearing outrageous drag (often called gender-fuck) to call attention to the absurdity of gender conformity. People in these groups may claim a gender-queer identity—that is, their gender is "queer" and does not fit into easily defined categories—but not identify as transgender. Like many transgender people, they see gender as a fluid spectrum. As trans activist Kate Bornstein has stated, "The opposite sex is neither." Many nontransgender people would agree with this too.

However people identify as transgender, they are confronted with decisions that non–trans-identified people never have to face. While it is often difficult for lesbian, gay, or bisexual people to come out, it is far more complicated for transgender people to explain their identities to friends and family. They frequently must deal with responses based in ignorance, confusion, or overt, even dangerous, hostility. Often they are asked very personal questions about their bodies or their sexual desires and activities. While there is a substantial body of popular and professional literature to help LGB people come out, there is very little available to transpeople.

Once people decide they are trans, no matter whom they tell, they must grapple with the question of how out they want to be. Do they want to pass as their actual—that is, experienced—gender, or remain "hidden" or cloaked in the sex they were assigned at birth? If they choose the first, they have to worry about how they appear to others through their clothing, personal demeanor, and emotional affect. If they choose the second—often for reasons of physical safety; visibly transpeople face an incredibly high risk of violence (see myth 15, "Transgender People Are Gay")—how difficult or healthy will it be to live splitting their core gender identity from their outward physical appearance? These decisions are both helped and made more difficult by ever-changing gender roles for nontranspeople. How do you change your gender in a world in which all gender roles are not as stable as they were in the past? Transpeople understand their gender psychologically, emotionally, and through their bodies. In this way, living as a transperson is a very complex embodied experience that most nontranspeople do not understand.

It is not surprising that in the past decade we have seen younger and younger people coming out as lesbian, gay, or bisexual, as well as transgender. This is due, to a large degree, to our society being more open to many more modes of gender identity and expression than ever before. On August 8, 2012, the *New York Times Magazine* published a long feature piece, "What's So Bad About a Boy Who Wants to Wear a Dress?," about young boys who expressed various forms of gender difference. (The author asserted, without argument, that it is much easier to be a gender-transgressive little girl.) The article openly and sympathetically described the problems faced by these boys and their families. It also painted an honest and nonjudgmental portrait of the boys and their wide range of experiences, noting how difficult it was to make sweeping social, medical, or cultural conclusions about their lives. Some boys eventually lost interest in "dressing up" as girls, and some did not. The article made clear that gender-variant behavior and identity were far less frightening to parents, and other adults, than they may have been a decade ago. The article also made clear that understanding, not panic or fear, was the most useful response to boys who expressed a desire to dress in girls' clothes, wear pink, and partake in traditionally female play. As one mother wrote on her blog, "It might make your world more tidy to have two neat and separate gender possibilities, but when you squish out the space between, you do not accurately represent lived reality. More than that, you're trying to 'squish out' my kid." This is an amazing cultural shift.

This shift is reflected in the scientific community, as well. The American Psychiatric Association has replaced the diagnosis gender identity disorder (with which some of the boys in the article had been diagnosed) with gender dysphoria to remove the stigma of disorder (see myth 6, "Transgender People Are Mentally Ill"). This is yet another sign that we as a culture are moving to a deeper understanding of the complexity of gender as it is lived and getting past the pathologization of transgender people.

So many factors beyond the medical arena influence transpeople's lives. For instance, because transgender experience and identity are shaped both by a longer history of transgenderism and by the particular cultural moment, generational divides between younger and older transpeople may be significant. Two decades ago, many of the boys profiled in the *New York Times Magazine* article would have been labeled as homosexual or psychologically disturbed—or possibly both—by the medical profession and even by their parents. There were no references to transgender children in medical literature before the mid-1990s; they were referred to as effeminate boys or masculine girls. But will preteens and teens who do not identify with their assigned gender see themselves as members of a transgender community? And if so, how? Who defines this community?

There will necessarily be countless divisions in this community because being trans can be defined in so many ways, and by so many people. For instance, if a person who identifies as a woman (after being assigned a male sex at birth) simply states that she is female and not trans, is she part of a self-identified trans community? If a person who easily passes as a man (after being assigned a female sex at birth) decides to "go stealth," is this person part of the trans community? Who gets to decide how transpeople look and act? Many older transpeople have voiced opposition to younger transpeople taking hormones, because they fear a public-opinion backlash against medical tampering with children's gender identity.[2] We do not know how younger transpeople coming out now may think about the lives and decisions made by the generations of transpeople who preceded them. We also don't know what tomorrow's generation of transpeople and genderqueers will think of today's gender rebels.

It is probably most useful to think of all gender as not only fluid but also on a broad spectrum of experience and appearance. Some transgender people are on the extreme end of that spectrum, others are more toward the middle. The decision to undergo sex-reassignment surgery is influenced by where you understand yourself to be on this spectrum. But for all people, the very idea of transgender allows for the attainment of a comfortable balance between your internal gender identity and how your body looks on the outside.

PART 2

CAUSE AND EFFECT

MYTH 4

SEXUAL ABUSE CAUSES HOMOSEXUALITY

The argument that homosexuality is the result of childhood sexual abuse is relatively new. Yet it has gained considerable currency over the past three decades. It is cited most frequently by religious and socially conservative groups, such as Heterosexuals Organized for a Moral Environment (HOME), who back up their claims with "academic" and "scientific" studies. HOME summarizes the all-encompassing conclusion of these studies by writing, "It is a well-documented fact that many, many homosexuals were sexually abused when young . . . we can see that sexual abuse can theoretically account for every case of homosexuality. . . ."[1]

The studies they quote have been overwhelmingly discounted by professional psychologists, who view them as junk science motivated by an extreme anti-LGBT agenda. The American Psychological Association has definitively stated that "to date there are no replicated scientific studies" that prove that a history of sexual abuse causes same-sex desires in women or men.[2] As popular as these discredited studies remain among many conservative groups, this myth did not originate with the studies. Both the myth and the studies reflect preexisting, though relatively recent, beliefs about homosexuality, and perhaps all sexual desire, that have made sexual abuse one of the go-to explanations whenever opponents of homosexuality seek to answer the question "What causes someone to become gay?"

The force of this myth, and its growing acceptance as common sense among large segments of the public in the past three decades, are a direct result of both the increased visibility of homosexuality and rising political gains of gay people during this same time. The myth's most vociferous proponents view the mere public presence of homosexuality as a threatening, overwhelming force whose political demands are inherently abusive to them and their values. They have transposed this personal sense of cultural shock onto the lives of LGB people to come up with the explanation that childhood sexual abuse must have caused their homosexuality. In addition to being wrong, this twisted logic is also a diminishment of the very real, widespread occurrence of sexual abuse. Like most traumatic experiences, sexual abuse does have the potential to influence a person's life, but how it does so varies from person to person and cannot be reduced to one story line.

The simplemindedness of this myth is self-evident. To the very complicated question "What causes homosexuality?" it poses a single, reductive answer: sexual abuse. A young girl who is sexually abused by a man becomes a lesbian because she has turned against men. A young boy who is abused by a man becomes homosexual because the abuse has programmed him to do so. This topsy-turvy logic aside, which predicts radically different results from an act of abuse—heterosexual abuse turns young females against men and into lesbians; homosexual abuse turns young males toward other men and makes them gay—what is unmistakably true is that sexual abuse is largely perpetrated by heterosexual men, although there is a small percentage done by women.

Many people argue that homosexuals are "born that way," and others argue that it is a choice (see myth 7, "Homosexuals Are Born That Way"). But this myth is very different. It is not about a person choosing homosexuality or being born gay, but more about what happens developmentally because of a sexual event that occurs during youth. To understand the larger social implications of this myth, and to see more clearly what animates it, we might restate the basic question as "How do human beings learn what and how they desire?"

As we explore our sexual desires, the actions we take, especially when they are pleasurable, may very well lead us to take more actions of a similar nature. Sexual expression is a learned experience, and we often learn by doing. People who view homosexuality as a sin or mental illness use this truism to make their point. Their panicked response begins with imagining any exposure to homosexuality as education in the wrong things and by the wrong people—which they then equate to sexual abuse to claim that actual sexual abuse causes homosexuality.

This is a vague but expansive argument that rests largely on our culture's misguided insistence that children are "innocent." To many adults, the belief in children's innocence means, above all, that children (perhaps especially their own) are devoid of all sexual feelings or interests. Because they are "innocent," simple exposure to the idea or reality of homosexuality, not necessarily a homosexual act, makes them "victims" (see myth 8, "LGBT Parents Are Bad for Children," and myth 16, "There's No Such Thing as a Gay or Trans Child"). The phrase "childhood sexual abuse" alone makes many people shudder. They cannot think of anything worse than an adult sexually abusing children. Equating simple exposure to the concept of homosexuality with actual sexual abuse gives this myth its power.

Ironically, the myth maintains its power because of heightened awareness of actual sexual abuse. In the past fifty years, Western culture has become increasingly aware of, and sensitive to, the reality that many children are physically, psychologically, and sexually abused by adults. Alongside this growing awareness has come the acknowledgment that abuse often has severe life consequences for the victim.

If the cultural power of the myth that sexual abuse causes homosexuality depended only on science, it would be as discredited as the studies that social conservatives keep quoting. Instead, the proponents of this myth have hinged their argument to the real incidence of sexual abuse, exploiting that reality to promote their anti-LGBT agenda.

Our culture portrays the tragedy of childhood sexual abuse all

31

the time. It is the premise of popular films such as *Sleepers* (1996) and *Mystic River* (2003) and is routinely featured in plotlines on crime-based television shows such as the various *Law and Order* series. There was even an entire reality television show, *To Catch a Predator* (2004–2007), predicated on sting operations that would trap men interested in having sex with teenagers. American culture is, in many ways, obsessed with child abuse, in particular, childhood sexual abuse. It is not surprising, then, that groups who want to attack LGBT people and their efforts to gain social freedom and basic equality under the law have quickly grasped for a connection between child sexual abuse and homosexuality.

With so many "ripped from the headlines" stories presented as fiction and so many real people unintentionally trapped in a sensationalized TV show that presented itself as activist journalism, it is clarifying to consider some facts about childhood sexual abuse. Most medical professionals define childhood sexual abuse as sexual activity, or the pressure to have sex, between an adult or an older adolescent and an underage person. But even this simple definition has to be qualified. In most states, the age of consent falls between sixteen and eighteen. People under this age cannot legally consent to sexual activity. If a person over the age of consent has sex with a person under that age, it is a crime. (The age restrictions vary from state to state.) Whether an age difference means the encounter is inherently abusive is an open question, especially since the law denies that the younger partner has any agency or desire in the encounter. Many people agree that, particularly for later adolescence, there should be a broader understanding, at least socially, around the ability for older teens to consent to sexual activity. Should a same-sex sexual encounter between a fourteen-year-old and a sixteen-year-old—two teenage boys fooling around—be considered sexual abuse of the younger teen when the age of consent is sixteen?

Not surprisingly, many of the studies that "prove" a link between childhood sexual abuse and homosexuality use a strict legal definition of abuse. If you are under the age of consent, you cannot consent, period. This is asserted as fact no matter how close in age you are to the person you had sex with and no matter your maturity and self-understanding. If the younger person ends up identifying as gay, such an encounter is "proof" of abuse causing homosexuality in the eyes of the people promoting this myth. What was completely consensual sex at the age of seventeen, and could surely have been important for the development of the "victim's" sexuality, can actually be considered sexual abuse under the law.[3]

There are many studies of the pervasiveness of childhood sexual abuse and who actually commits it. Studies differ in their findings. In 2009, *Clinical Psychology Review* conducted a review of sixty-five studies from twenty-two countries that looked at the incidence of childhood sexual abuse. They found that worldwide, 19.7 percent of women and 7.9 percent of men reported experiencing sexual abuse before they were eighteen. In the United States, the rates were 25.3 percent for women and 7.5 percent for men.[4] Most researchers agree that these figures are most likely vast undercounts; some studies show higher figures, also with the proviso that these involve undercounting as well. Research has shown that the likelihood of a child being sexually assaulted by a stranger is very low, probably 10 percent or under the number of reported instances. Acquaintances of the child's family account for 60 percent of the abuse, and 30 percent is perpetrated by people related to the child in some way.

Even though these figures are well established and accepted by a wide range of professionals in the medical and social-work fields, the myth still persists that a child is most endangered by random strangers and that gay men are the major perpetrators of child sexual abuse. The thinking here is quite simple and circular: (1) Sexual abuse of children is a crime, and crimes are committed by sexual criminals. (2) Homosexual acts have historically been criminalized, and although not criminalized now, are certainly considered by many people to be psychologically deviant and sinful. (3) Therefore, homosexuals are sexual criminals and, like other sexual criminals, must be committing these acts of abuse. The loop of this circular logic is closed by the further—and incorrect—argument that children who are sexually abused by homosexuals are destined to grow up to abuse others in the same way.

The myth that sexual abuse causes homosexuality first emerged in the late 1970s. The feminist movement of the time questioned not only gender roles but the structure of the nuclear family. Feminist thinkers such as Kate Millett and Shulamith Firestone flatly stated that children were an oppressed class of people. Firestone's chapter on children in her landmark *The Dialectic of Sex* is titled "Down with Childhood." Young people were organizing on their own behalf, and there were several national youth liberation movements that argued for greater freedom for young people, including young children. These ideas were disruptive to the status quo, and the government's response was to pass a series of laws intended to protect children, in particular the 1974 Child Abuse Prevention and Treatment Act. These laws also had the effect of disempowering children by treating them as passive and reinforcing their victimhood. The gay liberation movement, and later the LGBT rights movement, started after the Stonewall riots of 1969. All of this radical social change in such a condensed period of time created the perfect environment for the backlash against homosexuality to take the form of moral panics over endangered children.

Throughout the 1970s, the LGBT rights movement fought for and eventually won legal battles that allowed lesbians and gay men to be included under city and county laws that prohibited discrimination in employment, housing, and public accommodation based on race, ethnicity, religion, and national origin. In 1977, the commission for Florida's Miami-Dade County passed, by a 5 to 3 vote, such an antidiscrimination ordinance.

In response to this, Anita Bryant, a popular singer, Miss America runner-up, and devout Christian, formed Save Our Children, a political advocacy group with religious overtones, to overturn the ordinance through a referendum. Her main message was that this antidiscrimination ordinance would allow for openly lesbian and gay teachers to "recruit" children to homosexuality by simply offering the example of being openly homosexual or through overt sexual seduction. Despite a well-organized movement against it, her campaign was successful, and the referendum overturned the antidiscrimination ordinance by a margin of 69.3 percent to 30.6 percent.

Bryant's campaign spread to other cities, and many of the lesbian and gay antidiscrimination laws that had been passed in the 1970s were repealed. The lesbian and gay community organized again against this backlash. As a result, in 1978, when California state representative John Briggs introduced Proposition 6, which would have banned all lesbian and gay teachers from the state school system, citing similar concerns to Bryant's, it was defeated 58.4 percent to 41.6 percent.

Bryant and Briggs both argued that the intention of homosexuals' supposed abuse and molestation of children was specifically to make the children homosexuals. They also claimed that this abusive transformation could happen just by lesbian and gay men being open and visible, thus equating homosexual openness and visibility with an attack on childhood innocence. Implicit in all of this is the idea that the innocent child, if allowed to develop undisturbed by bad influences, will grow up to be heterosexual. Bryant stated, "What these people really want, hidden behind obscure legal phrases, is the legal right to propose to our children that theirs is an acceptable alternate way of life." This dramatic statement, while not mentioning childhood sexual abuse, inflates the logic underlying the myth that sexual abuse causes homosexuality. Homosexuality was such a threatening presence that it could overpower children's true heterosexual natures and make them gay. This was an abuse of nature, but more to the point, it was imagined as a usurpation of the parental right to control children's access to sexual information. Throughout the enormous national press coverage at the time, no one thought to ask lesbian and gay youth what they thought about their sexuality and why or how they came out as gay.

The context for this damaging argument was that American culture had become more accepting of gay and lesbian people and culture. Not only had the gay rights movement helped bring about significant legislation to ensure that discrimination would be addressed, many women and men were now coming out, and there were more images of gay people in films and on television. Bryant and Briggs used the rhetoric of child molestation, but their real concern was that young people might decide for themselves, in part due to the increase in "gay rights" and gay visibility, to come out as homosexual. Since they could not admit that some young people may actually be homosexual, they elaborated more and more on the myth that gay people molested children to make them homosexual. Intensely politicizing the situation, they resorted to war metaphors. Describing gay activists as "militant homosexuals," they accused them of recruiting children to their ranks. Bryant famously said, "As a mother, I know that homosexuals cannot biologically reproduce children; therefore, they must recruit our children."[5]

Since that time, the idea that lesbians and gay men recruit, seduce, lure, or trick young people into becoming homosexual has become more widespread and a hallmark of anti-LGBT rhetoric. The very concept of convincing or forcing young people to be gay against their nature is predicated on the idea that same-sex desire is inherently bad, as well as irresistible. For the people who make this argument, any sexual desire in children is a bad thing because it can overpower the person who experiences it.

The belief that heterosexuality is the only natural form of sexual attraction has led to the stigmatization of same-sex attraction as a particularly pernicious desire that somehow enters you from the world "out there." When people come out in their teens or younger, it is not only presumed that a gay person must have recruited, or abused, them, but that the very act of another person, especially an older person, saying, "I'm gay," has the force to make them gay as well. In addition to being absurd, this panicked logic diminishes the integrity and vibrancy of young people's sexuality and trivializes their ability to make healthy, informed, and pleasurable decisions about their own lives.

MYTH 5

MOST HOMOPHOBES ARE REPRESSED HOMOSEXUALS

"Oh, he is such a homophobe. He's probably really gay. That explains it." How often have you heard this? How often have you thought it? Ironically, appeals to common sense are usually made when logical explanations fail or when the explanation is just too confusing to make immediate sense. That is the case with this myth, and, perhaps, with the idea of homophobia itself. Society, culture, economics, power structures, family relationships, prejudices, religion, and so many other factors enter into the creation and maintenance of homophobia. Isolating any one factor, such as a person's supposed sexuality, and singling it out as the chief cause overlook this complexity. More important, with this myth, it also risks depoliticizing homophobia by turning it into a matter of one individual's warped psychology.

Furthermore, the word homophobia has become so broadly defined, and so broadly used, that it can refer to a staggeringly wide range of emotional states, from simple annoyance at the presence of homosexuals to murderous rage. There are enormous differences between these ends of the spectrum and everything in between. But one fact unites these emotional states: the wide application of homophobia to explain an entire gamut of negative reactions toward homosexuality is a direct result of the increasing visibility of social expressions of homosexuality.

The word "homophobia" is a recent invention. After the gay liberation movement began in the late 1960s, LGBT people and their allies needed some idea, and preferably one that matched their intuition, for how others could be so deeply repelled, and in so many different ways, by the increasing visibility of homosexuality. Psychologist George Weinberg coined "homophobia" in the late 1960s, and it was used intermittently by other writers until Weinberg popularized it in his 1972 book, *Society and the Healthy Homosexual.* Weinberg defined "homophobia" as the revulsion to, or fear of being in close contact with, a lesbian or gay man. Since that time it has become common usage—as well as generating similar terms such as biphobia and transphobia—and has decisively shaped the public discussion of how we think about emotions and actions that manifest animus against lesbians and gay men. Although "homophobia" may be a useful word in some instances, it is often immensely misleading in describing the hows and whys of people's feelings and actions. Nonetheless, many people made the connection that a fear of proximity to homosexuality somehow implicated a person in homosexuality.

This connection often feels intuitive. We have all experienced a situation when people hide something about which they feel ashamed, guilty, or nervous. They may begin to act defensively, or attempt to shift the blame, or shame, onto someone else. This is true of a five-year-old who is caught stealing a cookie from the kitchen after she should be in bed. Or of a co-worker who has not completed his assigned project on time and begins pointing fingers to shift the blame. It is easy to see how this reflexive emotional response might allow many people to think that when a person acts out or articulates a vivid homophobic response to a situation—say, reacting to the public presence of obviously gay men on a street by exclaiming loudly, "When did all the fags move into this neighborhood?"—that person might be hiding something about his own sexual desires. But maybe not. It is important to remember that the myth that most homophobes are repressed homosexuals is very often a story to explain and negate straight-male aggression against gay men.

In *Society and the Healthy Homosexual*, Weinberg argues, shockingly for the time, that homophobia is a common neurosis, or form of maladaptive, destructive behavior. Like other fears (*phobia* is the Greek word for fear)—such as those of being in tight spaces (claustrophobia), of being outside or in open spaces (agoraphobia), and of snakes (ophidiophobia; think of Indiana Jones)—homophobia is a mental imbalance and can severely limit personal interactions, as well as cause minor and major disruptions to an individual's experience of the world. (Obviously, homophobia also causes minor and major disruptions for the lesbians and gay men who are its victims.)

Homophobia, according to Weinberg, is a symptom of deeper prejudice that gains its meaning and power from the ways individuals fear people different from themselves. Weinberg locates the roots of homophobia in specific moral and political views about the world, including religious beliefs that homosexual acts are sinful and the idea that nonheterosexual behavior is a threat to traditional values. Racism is similarly influenced and constructed by a long, complicated history in the United States and is entwined with legal, social, and economic issues. Although Weinberg wrote that the fear of "being homosexual" was about much more than homosexuality per se, the connection between the fear of gay people and the fear of being gay yourself rang so true to readers that it became the main idea people took away from the book. And it quickly became ingrained in both LGBT and mainstream culture.

But Weinberg did not claim that the people who feared homosexuals most—and, again, he was writing almost entirely about men fearing other men—were repressed homosexuals. Human beings are capable of a wide range of erotic feelings. Heterosexuals can feel conflicted about their same-sex attractions, but so can people primarily attracted to the same sex. None of these internal conflicts would be extraordinary, since our culture—even now, which is far more accepting than in the past—does not encourage individuals to understand, and be comfortable with, their sexual desires. We are taught not to explore or express them. In his 1948 study *Sexual Behavior in the Human Male*, Alfred Kinsey and his team of researchers wrote, "The anatomy and functional capacities of male genitalia interest the younger boy to a degree that is not appreciated by older males who have become heterosexually conditioned and who are continuously on the defensive against reactions which might be interpreted as homosexual."[1] Weinberg noted a similar defense. Whether predominantly heterosexual or homosexual, people who are not comfortable with their same-sex attractions may try to negate these desires through what Weinberg calls "chronic self-denial." He also argued that people with deep unhappiness about this conflict may experience a "flight into guilt."[2] Both of these results might be described as "repressing" same-sex erotic attractions because they make these people feel uncomfortable, nervous, and even panicked when confronted with homosexual people of the same sex as themselves.

These psychological responses reflect some of the social and political realities with which we all live. Repression is not simply an internal process. Repression is a response to an entire social world. Homosexuality comes to have meaning, whether pleasant or uncomfortable, only because it is viewed and understood through that world. A person cannot repress "homosexuality" as such because it is not an entity with clear boundaries. It would be absurd to argue that all white racists secretly think they are black or want to be black. The "repression of homosexuality" is the repression of a whole string of associated ideas that for one person may connect to same-sex attraction. Another person may have different associations. We all repress, to some degree, aspects of our erotic desires, sometimes because they are culturally frowned upon, but also because they can be associated with feelings that make us uncomfortable. When something in this repressed chain is drudged up by a reminder of it in daily life, we need to get rid of the discomfort it causes. This is why it makes sense to people that acts of violent homophobia are due to the repression of homosexual tendencies.

Another persuasive aspect of this myth is that it reinforces the widespread cultural fantasy that heterosexual men are unfazed by the possibility of same-sex desire. In this fantasy "real" straight men are so secure in their heterosexuality that they would never need to act out against gay people and, especially, gay men. It is insecure straight men, and closeted gay men, who are the problem. Heterosexual men thus have no connection to, or blame for, homophobic violence.

Rather than homophobes repressing their homosexual feelings, it is more likely that they are avoiding the idea of homosexuality. In his 1946 foundational study of prejudice, *Anti-Semite and Jew*, Jean-Paul Sartre, writing just after the Holocaust, boldly argues that anti-Semitism has less to do with Jews than with the fragile psyche and identity of the anti-Semite.

The anti-Semite has essentially created a fantastical idea of the Jew (which has nothing to do with actual people or culture) that "explains" everything that is wrong with both the society in which the anti-Semite lives as well as his own life. In the anti-Semite's fervid imagination, the mythical Jew has too much social power, controls the banks and national wealth, and controls cultural institutions such as universities. In its most extreme version, the anti-Semite imagines that "the Jew" conspires against Christians, molesting and murdering Christian children. This fantasy Jew, which Sartre called "the idea of the Jew," becomes the scapegoat for all that is wrong with the world. Sartre further argues that anti-Semitism is not an "opinion," that is, a view based upon facts, but a "passion," which is deeply believed despite all facts to the contrary. When the anti-Semite is even fleetingly reminded of this "Jew," he feels entitled to react, sometimes violently, with a strongly felt anti-Semitism, telling himself that he is only defending himself and his culture, not attacking another person or group.

Sartre's ideas strike home today. Homophobic passion, impervious to facts, is spouted by many evangelical Christians. Does this mean that televangelists such as Pat Robertson or the late Jerry Falwell, whose pronouncements about homosexuality are extreme

and do great damage, are closeted homosexuals? Their homophobic diatribes can be so sexually explicit a listener might think these
men were intimately familiar with homosexuality. It is tempting to
say that this familiarity indicates that they are secretly gay. But it
makes more sense to say that their relationship to homosexuality
is complicated, and like Sartre's anti-Semite, makes sense of their
world. Robertson has used homosexuality to explain earthquakes
and Hurricane Katrina. This is completely illogical, but passion is
not logical. It is possible that homophobes may be envious of the
pleasure they deny themselves. This pleasure is then projected
onto the sinful homosexual. A recurrent theme in most antigay
jeremiads is that gay men are wildly promiscuous and engage in
outré sexual acts. Here the idea of the homosexual, not actual homosexuals, represents forbidden pleasures. Just as Jews historically
are associated with money, homosexuals have become associated
with sex. Wild, out-of-control sex becomes the very meaning of
homosexuality. In a culture that does not deal honestly with pleasure, and in which sex is sometimes depicted as a biological force
that leads to social anarchy if not properly controlled, the fantasy
of the sex-crazed homosexual can generate intense social and
personal antagonism.

Many homophobes trumpet family values that explicitly exclude
gay and lesbian people. This rhetoric is a continuation of the fantasy world of the post–World War II suburban American Dream. It
was during this time that the increasing visibility of homosexuals in
US culture began to lead to increased social tensions around sexuality. Many women and men came home from the war and moved
to cities to live openly homosexual lives. This instigated widespread
fears that homosexuals were a subversive danger to a productive society and national security. The promotion of traditional models of
behavior, such as the heterosexual nuclear family with clearly defined gender roles, was a response to this threat. There was also a
political response to the homosexual threat. Anticommunist witch
hunts, like those organized by Senator Joseph McCarthy, defini-

tively associated communism with homosexuality. As a result, thousands of gay men and lesbians were fired from their government jobs because they were believed to be security risks who could be blackmailed for whatever secrets they held. The witch-hunting homophobe was part of, in historian Richard Hofstadter's phrase, "the paranoid style in American politics."

Recent scientific studies have attempted to prove the connection between homophobic attitudes and repressed homosexuality. One study, "Is Homophobia Associated with Homosexual Arousal?" (1996), assessed the level of homophobia in white, heterosexually identified, male college students through questionnaires, and then tested whether they were aroused by gay porn by attaching a plethysmograph to measure the engorgement of their penis. The men who had been identified as homophobic were twice as likely to have a penile response to the gay porn, yet were also either unaware of their physiological response or denied it. Media reports trumpeted the study as proving that repressed same-sex attraction caused homophobia. But this was a serious misreading. The study did not prove that these "homophobic" males were secretly turned on by male homosexuality. Or that they were homosexual themselves. All this study demonstrated was that their homosexual arousal could occur as a result of the very anxiety around its possibility. Whether they were already attracted to the same sex is a different question.

A 2012 series of studies of 164 students from the United States and Germany also identified homophobia through a series of questions. But these studies used answers to additional questions, rather than physiological changes, to assess arousal in response to both sexual and nonsexual images. The studies concluded that "homophobia is more pronounced in individuals with an unacknowledged attraction to the same sex and who grew up with authoritarian parents who forbade such desires." What the series actually demonstrates, however, is that homophobic responses are never just psychological or personal, but also always cultural, social, and maybe political.

These homophobia studies received a huge amount of media attention when they were published. The press release for the second string of studies claimed that it

> sheds light on high profile cases in which anti-gay public figures are caught engaging in same-sex sexual acts [including that of] Ted Haggard, the evangelical preacher who opposed gay marriage but was exposed in a gay sex scandal in 2006, and Glenn Murphy, Jr., former chairman of the Young Republican National Federation and vocal opponent of gay marriage, who was accused of sexually assaulting a 22-year-old man in 2007.[3]

Such extrapolations are absurd. No one explanation of homophobia, whether it is a political position or a scientific measurement, can be fully accurate if it denies its connections to the many other frames through which we see the world.

Whatever the complications of each individual psyche, we all live in a world that influences us every day in myriad ways. Homophobia, in all of its forms, expresses real social anxieties over how something will fit in or disrupt the world "as it is." But that world is seen differently by every individual in it. That's its trouble and its promise.

MYTH 6

TRANSGENDER PEOPLE ARE MENTALLY ILL

Like lesbians, gay men, and bisexuals, transgender people have long struggled under the burden of being labeled mentally disordered or diseased. The simple answer to the question of whether transgender people suffer from a mental disorder is, no, they do not. But the reality of living as a transgender person is not simple, and there are some transgender activists and allies who believe there is an ongoing utility to labeling transgender as a medical disorder of some kind.

There are different theories, but no scientific consensus, about what causes people to feel that their gender identity does not fit with the sex they were assigned at birth. Some scientists stress biological factors, arguing that hormonal fluctuations in utero may play a role. Other explanations have focused on "psychogenic" factors, such as how familial and psychological dynamics shape gender identity. Increasingly, physicians and psychiatrists understand transgenderism to be a normal variation in the way some people experience their bodies and their selves as gendered individuals. From this perspective, transgenderism is not a condition that needs to be cured. And it is certainly not—as terms such as "mental disorder" suggest—a pathology. Rather, it is an identity or just a sense of felt experience that requires acceptance and support.

Affirmation of transgender life and experience has been hard-won, and remains an ongoing struggle. The idea that transpeople are not "sick" is still not universally accepted in the medical and psychiatric communities. Nor is it necessarily accepted by American society.

The belief that transgenderism is a mental disorder makes it easier for some nontransgender people to understand transgender people's accounts of feeling they are in the wrong body. But what does it mean to feel like you are in the wrong body, that the sex assigned to you at birth does not accord with the gender identity you feel inside? Transgender activists would turn this question around and ask nontransgender people, What does it feel like to be in the right body, and how do you know?

There is a long history to the question of who is authorized to speak about, or for, transgender people and what role medical knowledge plays in defining transgenderism. This history overlaps with some key medical debates over homosexuality. Well into the twentieth century, homosexuality continued to be classified as a mental disorder and was labeled as such in the *Diagnostic and Statistical Manual of Mental Disorders (DSM)*. The *DSM*, first published in 1952, is the professional handbook for psychiatrists, psychotherapists, and—crucially—insurers. It identifies and classifies "disorders," their causes, their standard treatments, and the likelihood of cure. It is painstakingly revised approximately every fifteen years to reflect changing understandings of mental disorders and available treatments. In the first two editions, homosexuality was listed as a mental disorder. In 1973, LGB activists and their allies in mental health communities succeeded in having it declassified as a pathology.

Nearly four decades later, transgender activists confronted a similar dilemma. They needed to undo the harmful stigmas resulting from being labeled, and treated, as a disordered identity. In 1980, the third edition of the *DSM* described transsexualism in adults and significant gender nonconformity in children as mental disturbances. Previously, transsexualism in adults was not listed as a separate disorder, and there was no diagnosis for gender-nonconforming children. *DSM-III* was also the first edition in which homosexuality per se did not appear as a mental disorder. Some LGBT activists have speculated that gender identity disorder in childhood—the diagnosis given to gender nonconforming children, and especially to nonconforming boys—was a deliberate attempt to get homosexuality back onto the list of mental disorders by pathologizing young sissies.[1]

The fourth edition of the *DSM*, in 1994, presented a unified diagnosis, gender identity disorder (GID), which could manifest in adults, adolescents, and children.[2] ("Transgender" is not a medical term and nowhere appears in the *DSM*.) The recommended treatments for GID varied depending on the age of the person. GID's indicators were "a strong persistent cross-gender identification (not merely a desire for any perceived cultural advantages of being the other sex)" and an individual's "persistent discomfort with his or her sex or sense of inappropriateness in the gender role of that sex." The *DSM-IV*'s diagnostic criteria also considered social impact and required evidence that "the disturbance causes clinically significant distress or impairment in social, occupational, or other important areas of functioning."

Transgender activists and allies protested gender identity disorder, claiming it stigmatized transgender identity. Many transgender people do suffer profound distress because of the incongruence between how they perceive themselves—their core gender identity—and their assigned sex. They do not feel at home in the bodies they were born into. This experience of self-estrangement can lead to suicidal depression and other serious emotional distress. However, these emotional problems are not caused by a transgender person's core identity but by the embodied or felt tension between this core identity and the sex assigned at birth. This distress can start at a young age. Although trans children might not be immediately diagnosed with GID, they could easily be seen by family, friends, and physicians as "different" or "special."

In other societies, "different" and "special" can be positive, even honored attributes. Many nonwestern cultures have historically created room for a third sex or third gender, individuals who are seen as falling in between the two biological sexes or who embody the gendered qualities of both.[3] The *hijras* of South Asia are an example of a culturally and legally recognized third gender. The berdache of some Native American traditions are another. Such third-sex individuals are frequently assigned crucial ritualistic roles in their societies as priests or priestesses, shamans, or intermediaries between deities and humans. Transgender adults and children in the United States are not asking to be given a special role; they want to be allowed to live their lives and have access to the trans-specific medical care they need—all without being told they are a problem to be solved.

Transpeople need equal access to general health care as well as access to trans-specific care. The latter may take several forms. Some transpeople who feel "persistent discomfort" in their assigned sex may want medical interventions to change their bodies— this is called transitioning. This process could include removing the breasts (known as "top surgery") or surgically changing the genitals ("bottom surgery"). Other transpeople may want hormone treatment, which will allow them to change secondary sexual characteristics and more easily pass as their inner, experienced gender (see myth 3, "All Transgender People Have Sex-Reassignment Surgery").

Many transpeople rely on psychotherapy to deal with "clinically significant distress." Their experience of "impairment in social, occupational, or other important areas of functioning" is a direct result of widespread prejudice and legal discrimination. In most US states, it is legal to fire people or refuse to rent them an apartment because of their gender identity (see myth 19, "Antidiscrimination Laws Protect LGBT People"). Transpeople are frequently targets of violent hate crimes because of their gender nonconformity. There are thus many reasons for transgender people to manifest "clinically significant distress." It is very difficult to separate the distress resulting from the tension between gender identity and assigned sex and the distress experienced from external pressures such as prejudice. For some transpeople, the former could be the internalized version of the latter. That is, other people's negative judgments about transgenderism can get transformed into a transperson's internal experience of shame or "badness."

In addition to contributing to social stigma and prejudice, the diagnosis gender identity disorder also creates legal disadvantages. Legal advocates point to many instances in which transpeople were at risk of losing custody of their children because they were labeled "mentally ill." Such reasoning could affect employment, as well. Trans activists have worked to change how psychiatry and medicine look at transgender identity, focusing on the enormous influence of the *DSM*. When the American Psychiatric Association began work on the *DSM-V*, published in 2013, it formed a working group of psychiatrists to reconsider the current diagnosis, treatment recommendations, and nomenclature for gender identity disorder. Transgender advocates formed their own working groups, wrote policy papers, and made recommendations, too, so that their concerns would be taken into account.

The *DSM-V* represents a victory for transgender people and their allies. References to gender identity disorder have been dropped. Instead, *DSM-V* now lists gender dysphoria, which applies only if a transperson's experience of gender incongruity causes significant distress to him or her. Not all transpeople experience this kind of distress, so the new diagnosis creates space for different experiences and desired embodiments among transgender people. Gender dysphoria also applies in cases where a transperson's situation impairs basic life needs, such as holding a job or securing housing.

Many trans activists wanted all references to transgender experience deleted from the *DSM*. Transgenderism, they argued, was not a medical problem. Decisively separating trans from categorization as a medical problem or condition could certainly help pave the way toward recognizing it as simply a normal variation of human gender identity and experience. Unfortunately, American society cannot accept this yet. More important, transgender health-care advocates in the United States and internationally have made a compelling case for why transgenderism should be in the *DSM* in some form. Their argument is that some kind of medical diagnosis is often necessary for transpeople to access the many types of medical care they need for transitioning or taking hormones. Without a psychiatric diagnosis attesting to a transperson's persistent sense of incongruence between gender identity and body, the few insurers that will cover medical transitions might no longer do so. Additionally, many medical professionals would be unwilling to offer transgender people transition-specific care, even if they were paying out of pocket, because there was no medically recognized condition to treat.

During the debate over *DSM-V*, legal advocates for transgender people expressed concerns about how declassification of gender identity disorder might affect transpeople in other areas, as well. Lambda Legal Defense argued that when transgender people in the United States want to change their legal name and sex on state documents, such as licenses and birth certificates, they often need to provide a doctor's statement that they live full-time in their experienced gender identity. Frequently, this medical documentation requires a psychiatric diagnosis of some kind. Without it, Lambda points out, transpeople may find their legal and health-care options limited. This would be a very dangerous outcome for transpeople, whose options are already highly limited. In the name of freeing transpeople from the stigma of mental illness, other unintended harms may follow.

The new diagnosis of gender dysphoria thus represents a pragmatic and destigmatizing compromise. In an ideal world, the vast multitude of genders would be recognized and legitimated with equal social benefits, including access to comprehensive physical and mental health care. At the same time, the distress caused by the difficulty or unwillingness to uphold gender norms can be real, and serious, for any individual, not just transpeople. This is equally true of the struggle many people may have around their sexuality. The *DSM* also lists a sexuality dysphoria, although it is not categorized under that name. But we know that such an experience, whether applied to gender or sexuality, is common in less acute but no less insidious forms in the contemporary United States.

The reality is that we, as a society, lack a useful, comprehensive language for mental distresses of all kinds. We are afraid, or ashamed, to speak about them. We are often afraid to discuss our own fears and problems. All too often we use mental illness as an easy way to compartmentalize and discuss people to place their problems and lives into neat little boxes. This makes us feel "healthy" and "normal." Given the cultural confusion about transgender identity and gender fluidity, is it any surprise that terms such as "gender identity disorder" and "gender dysphoria" can make nontransgender people feel comfortable about those "other" people?

Our languages—whether medical, legal, or everyday—for talking about and naming gender identity have not kept pace with the diversity of ways in which people are already experiencing and expressing their gender identity, whether they identify as trans or not. Maybe what we as a culture need to think about is not how to label others, but how all of our gender and sexual identities do not perfectly fit the prescribed norms. Doing this may make others' lives—and our own—a little easier.

MYTH 7

HOMOSEXUALS ARE BORN THAT WAY

Award-winning and openly lesbian actress Cynthia Nixon landed herself in hot water—twice. Her missteps? Nixon, best known for playing brainy and neurotic Miranda on *Sex in the City*, stated, in her acceptance of GLAAD's Vito Russo Award in March 2010, "I've been straight and I've been gay, and gay is better."[1] LGBT advocates objected to the implication that homosexuality was a choice. In a January 2012 interview with the *New York Times*, Nixon unapologetically stood her ground: "For me, it is a choice. I understand that for many people it's not, but for me it's a choice, and you don't get to define my gayness for me." Nixon's words went viral.

Since the Stonewall riots in 1969, LGB activists have encouraged gay people to come out and speak the truth about their lives. Why were activists so angry with Nixon for boldly telling her own truth? What political, and personal, nerve had she inadvertently struck?

In the past decade, the argument that homosexuals are born that way has become a major talking point used by LGB advocates to argue for equal rights. Nixon's declaration, "For me, it's a choice," strayed from this carefully crafted political and legal script. Worse, it could be heard as reinforcing the antigay message of some conservative political groups. These groups, in their own public relations strategy, describe homosexuality as a "lifestyle choice" or "behavior-based identity." If being gay is a "choice," it supposedly does not merit the civil rights protections extended to racial minorities and women.

But "born that way" is more than a sound bite in a public relations war. Many LGB people describe their sexual identities as inborn, an immutable part of who they are. Some others, like Nixon, claim they choose to be gay. This may be particularly true for lesbians. In the late 1970s, some feminists believed lesbianism was a chosen political and sexual identity. These "political lesbians" did not necessarily have sex with, or even sexually desire, women. Most self-declared lesbians decidedly do desire and have sex with other women (see myth 13, "Lesbians Do Not Have Real Sex").

Still other LGB people would say their sexuality is both chosen and unchosen. They may not have chosen their same-sex desires, but they do choose to act on them and come out as L, G, or B. Other LGB people would say they do not care how or why they came to be gay—they are gay and it is fine. LGB people, like straight people, have all sorts of ways of answering the question, "Why are you the way you are?"

Sexuality, or the life of desire, asks profound questions about relating to others in the world we share. The intricacies of sexual desire, especially whom we desire, have been understood as an important key to who we are since "homosexuality" and "heterosexuality" were invented as distinct identities in the mid-nineteenth century. Yet in the contemporary United States—because heterosexuality is presumed to be the natural, default position—all the pressure is on LGB people to explain their desires and justify their existence. This has meant that LGB people's explanations for who and why they are acquire disproportionately large moral, legal, and personal significance.

What is the connection between whether or not LGB people are born gay and whether they should be protected from discrimination? If LGB people are born that way, and cannot change who they are, it would be unjust to discriminate against them. Alternately, if homosexuality is a choice, then society is not required to extend equal protections to LGB people as a group. This latter argument implies that homosexuality is not just a choice, but a bad choice. Ironically, the gay-affirming, born-that-way argument may imply this as well. Defending homosexuality on the grounds that LGB people are born that way and just can't help it could bolster the idea that there is something wrong with being L, G, or B.

This discussion raises several issues that need to be addressed. When it comes to the moral question of how to treat other people in everyday interactions, it does not matter what causes homosexuality. There is nothing wrong with same-sex desire or LGB lives.

Second, LGB people deserve equal protection under the law. As a simple matter of fairness and legal precedent, it does not matter whether homosexuality is "immutable." This is not a legal requirement for granting equal rights.

Finally, it is simply not true that heterosexuality is the way everyone naturally is. We know from studies that a large number of heterosexually identified people have had same-sex sexual relations at some point in their lives (see myth 2, "About 10 Percent of People Are Gay or Lesbian"). Heterosexuality does not occupy a moral high ground of naturalness. It is also as much in need of explanation as homosexuality.

Attempts to explain what causes homosexuality have a long, and often ugly, history. Various medical theories that pathologized homosexuality have caused and justified outright violence against LGB people, most notably, the use of electroshock treatments as part of therapeutic attempts to cure homosexuality in the 1950s. As terrible as this history is, it does not mean that attempts to consider what causes homosexuality—or how it evolves—are necessarily bad or dangerous for LGB people.

All scientific studies are carried out by humans and are never free of cultural assumptions and even prejudice. This may be especially so for scientific attempts to explain sexuality and its causes. Historically, the science of human desire has been deeply connected to impassioned debates over the morality of homosexuality. Many scientists have pursued this research because they held strong views one way or another.

The nineteenth-century invention of the homosexual and the heterosexual as distinct kinds of persons was followed almost immediately by various scientific attempts to explain why some women and men desire their own sex. Karl Heinrich Ulrichs was an influential early thinker who argued that the male homosexual had the body of a man and the soul of a woman, and that the reverse was true for a lesbian. This scientific explanation seems naive and misguided to us today, but it was an important step in giving people a way to think about the origins of their sexual desires (see myth 15, "Transgender People Are Gay").

A growing body of contemporary scientific research suggests that sexual desire—both gay and straight—may be related to brain structure. The most widely publicized such study is Simon LeVay's 1991 study of "the hypothalamus, which controls the release of sex hormones from the pituitary gland." His study claimed the hypothalamus "in gay men differs from the hypothalamus in straight men. The third interstitial nucleus of the anterior hypothalamus (INAH3) was found to be more than twice as large in heterosexual men as in homosexual men."[2] LeVay's research garnered front-page coverage in the *New York Times*. The ensuing criticisms of LeVay's study—many by other scientists—received far less attention.

Along with his survey sample being too small for an accurate study, his basic assumption that male/female brain differences are comparable to gay/straight differences—assumptions oddly similar to Ulrich's—made little sense. Additionally, he never took into consideration the lived sexuality and experiences of his subjects.

Other brain research has been examining how "exposure to sex hormones in the womb during a critical period in brain development affects future sexual orientation."[3] These studies also suffer from a confused set of assumptions. Historian of science Rebecca Jordan-Young notes that, "Sexuality is notoriously hard to define. So when a headline proclaims, 'Prenatal Environment May Dictate Sexual Orientation,' just what is it, exactly, that it is said to have dictated? Is it whom someone desires? Whom one has sex with? What a person calls him or herself?"[4] The rigid models and language used by these studies—male/female and heterosexual/homosexual—cannot capture the multidimensional character of sexuality.

Genetic studies of sexual desire appear at first less problematic. Scientists have hypothesized that homosexuality runs in families. Studies done on twins seem to support this, finding that the identical twin of a lesbian has almost a 50 percent likelihood of being lesbian herself. A similar correlation—or concordance rate—was observed in cases of gay men with an identical twin brother. Concordance rates were lower, but still significant, in cases of fraternal twins and nontwin siblings. Identical twins share 100 percent of their genetic material, fraternal and nontwin siblings, approximately 50 percent. These differing rates are consistent with the idea that there is some genetic component to homosexuality.[5]

Although these studies demonstrate that there may be a genetic basis to homosexuality, none of the studies has explained how this works. Genetic studies give us a picture of associations, but not the direct genetic mechanism by which genetic inheritance could "cause" homosexuality.[6]

Genes also never operate in isolation from environment. Except in extreme circumstances (such as twins separated at birth), identical twins, fraternal twins, and even nontwin genetic siblings share many of the same childhood environmental factors. They share the same house, attend the same schools, watch the same TV shows, and have the same parental and adult role models.[7] If it is difficult to separate biology from environment, we also need to remember that biological capacities develop in relation to their environments. For example, many people dislike a specific food on their first encounter, only to have it become a favorite treat later on. The biological ability to digest this food was always there, but the taste for it had to be cultivated. Sexual preferences may operate along similar lines. Biological capacities and, possibly, biological predispositions become focused in different ways, depending on complex environmental factors.[8]

Still, environment can only take us so far in trying to answer the questions "Why am I the way I am?" and "Why do I like what I like?" The twin studies demonstrate that identical twins share 100 percent of their genetic material and may share, as children, very similar environments. But twin homosexuals exist in only 50 percent of the cases. Clearly, neither genetics, nor genetics plus environment, can tell the whole story.[9]

For much of the twentieth century, the most influential scientific theories concerning homosexuality came from psychiatry and psychology. These theories, importantly, introduced the idea that individuals play some role in the formation of their sexuality, even as they are always doing so in relation to others and to a larger culture.

Sigmund Freud, the founding father of psychoanalysis, thought that homosexuality was a normal variation of human sexual desire. He also thought that all people experienced, at least unconsciously, desire for the same sex at some point in their lives.[10] Nonetheless, he believed that sexual development should end in reproductive heterosexuality, and in some of his writings portrayed homosexuality as a detour from that end point, an arrested development. But he also consistently argued that the path to reproductive heterosexuality was so difficult for anyone that it could not happen without compromise. In order to achieve mature reproductive heterosexuality, individuals have to restrict—give up—the much wider range of ways their desires might be experienced and expressed. Desires are shaped by cultural norms but not fully determined or "caused" by them. This insight is one of the reasons why Freud spent much more of his work explaining how people become "heterosexual."

The unconscious is one of the great discoveries of psychoanalysis. We can see its workings in any number of ways, such as in how we connect memories and what appears in our dreams. With desire, we can glimpse the unconscious in the disconnect that often occurs between what we say we want in a sexual partner or lover and the kind of person we actually choose (often, over and over again). The unconscious helps explain the fact that the formation and expression of human desire are never fully within our control, nor even within our conscious understanding. Our desire always contains more than we could ever know, let alone admit or tell.

Freud's ideas about sexuality were often contradictory. Some of them reinforced false ideas about gay people. Others greatly expanded the bounds of what people thought was sexually "normal" to include a wide range of desires, fantasies, acts, and self-understandings. But Freud's psychiatric followers in the United States ignored his subtle, subversive claims about homosexuality, heterosexuality, and the unconscious life of desire. Spurred on by the political and social conservatism of post–World War II America, they selectively grafted his theory of homosexuality onto a model of mental pathology. In 1952, the first edition of the *Diagnostic and Statistical Manual of Mental Disorders (DSM)* called homosexuality a "sociopathic personality disorder."

One of the most influential proponents of the pathology theory was psychiatrist Irving Bieber, who argued, in 1962, that "heterosexuality is the biologic norm and . . . unless interfered with all individuals are heterosexual."[11] Bieber identified the "causes" of homosexuality as negligent parenting, or other dangerous environmental factors such as society's glamorization of homosexuality. Another prominent psychiatrist, Fredric Wertham, argued in his 1954 *Seduction of the Innocent* that Batman and Robin were coded homosexual lovers and Wonder Woman was a man-hating lesbian. (Wertham also testified at a congressional hearing that comic books corrupted young people and led to juvenile delinquency.) While images of LGB people in the media do shape people's imaginations of what is possible to express about themselves, they do not do so in this simplistic way (see myth 4, "Sexual Abuse Causes Homosexuality").

Psychiatrists such as Bieber argued that they could "cure" homosexuals through therapy, an idea still with us today. Sometimes this takes the form of so-called conversion, or reparative therapy, promoted by many conservative religious groups. Another, more strictly religious version of this is to pray for God to cure you, often referred to as "pray the gay away." But even here, major changes are underway. In 2013, in a surprise move, Exodus International, the world's oldest and largest evangelical Christian ministry dedicated to helping gay men and lesbians find "alternatives" to unwanted same-sex attractions, disbanded and publicly apologized for perpetuating shame, false hope, and trauma.

Although other ex-gay ministries remain committed to curing same-sex attraction, no reputable scientific studies support any of this. Not the bad-parenting theory. Not the indoctrination model. And certainly not the idea that homosexuality can be cured. This negative view of homosexuality very slowly came to an end for a variety of reasons. New research, such as Evelyn Hooker's important 1957 study showing that homosexuals were no more likely to suffer from psychopathologies than heterosexuals, changed the mind of medical professionals. Society's views were also changing during this time. Most important, the gay liberation movement—and other activists speaking the truth about their own lives—demanded change. In 1973, the American Psychiatric Association reversed its decades-long stance and dropped its categorization of homosexuality per se as a disorder from the *DSM*. Irving Bieber and other conservative psychiatrists fought against this change and, for the next decades, also spoke out against the gay rights movement. But it is now the overwhelming consensus of "the behavioral and social sciences and the health and mental health professions" that homosexuality is, to quote the American Psychological Association, "a normal and positive variation of human sexual orientation."

So, if there is no proof that homosexuals are biologically born that way, or that they are made that way through unhealthy parenting or bad cultural influences, then maybe Cynthia Nixon is right: individual agency is the real question, and people do just choose to be gay or lesbian.

The question of "born that way" versus "choice" is much more complex than either the political debates or scientific studies generally admit. The problem is that to many people, the word "cause"—

like "choice" and "born that way"—marks a kind of big bang theory of sexuality that explains everything about who we are and how our sexual desire works.

It is more useful to think about cause as the more expansive question of how a person comes to have a character, or a personality. Sexuality is not a containable part of yourself, or simply reducible to a sex act. Rather, it is an ongoing process formed by the interactions of our psyche, body, and environment. Both we, as individuals, and the world around us are implicated. Sexuality, like personality, is a product of a string of minute choices—wanted, forced, compromised—that we consciously and unconsciously make during our endless negotiations of the world into which we are born. We can never know the precise moment when a person becomes gay. Nor can we know exactly how or why it happens. The same can be said about when, how, or why a person becomes straight.

Every day we make decisions, both direct and indirect, that lead to consequences we may never intend—but which we may come to understand and experience as profoundly desirable. For example, a young woman who attends a women's college may encounter a vibrant community of lesbian, bi, and queer women. Perhaps this opens up possibilities for her own desire she did not know she had—possibilities she might not have discovered, or admitted, had she chosen a co-ed school. Her choices affected the path of her desire and self-identification; but, so did the countless other turns she took from the moment she was born, turns that also inevitably involved her in the lives of others. (In this instance, these turns include getting into, and affording, a private college.)

To ask what causes homosexuality is to try to understand how we, as humans, learn to grapple with a world of ultimately unanswerable mysteries—including the mystery of our own desire. This mystery entangles us in other vital questions: how our feelings and relationships come to have the meanings they do. How community results from these actions. And how we come to survive and live productively within it all.

PART 3

TROUBLEMAKERS

MYTH 8

LGBT PARENTS ARE
BAD FOR CHILDREN

All the evidence is clear: same-sex or transgender parents in two-parent or single-parent families can be great parents, good parents, indifferent parents, or bad parents. Just like heterosexual parents. Whether they are attracted to men or women has nothing to do with it. This is why almost every national psychological and social work professional organization—including the American Psychological Association, the American Academy of Pediatrics, the National Association of Social Workers, and the Child Welfare League of America—have publicly stated that there is no harm done to children by lesbian or gay male parents. (There are no statistics or professional statements yet on transgender parents, but the questions surrounding their parenting overlap with those of lesbian and gay male parents.)

Nevertheless, the myth that LGBT parents are somehow bad, or dangerous, for children remains deeply embedded in our culture. The primary reason has to do with the way our culture thinks about sexual identity. Both sides in this debate, those defending LGBT parenting and those attacking it, foreground the sexual identity of LGBT parents. One side says it does not matter; the other side insists it does, dangerously so. Either way, the debate never gets past sexual identity. This is a problem if we want to have a more complex conversation about the realities of LGBT parenting.

The power of this myth rests on the idea that parent is itself an identity and, for many people, an all-encompassing one. But parent is not an identity. It names a social relation between a child and his or her caretaker. In some similar ways, sexual identity is only one aspect of sexuality. When we focus on whether a certain identity—such as lesbian, gay, bisexual, transgender, or straight—is more acceptable and less harmful than another, we miss the point. It is not identity, but rather the complications of lived experience and lived relationships that affect people's lives. When parenting is at question, those interpersonal complications can indeed harm children, no matter the "identity" of the parent or parents.

The idea that sexual identity is a predominant problem in parenting shapes arguments against same-sex marriage, LGBT people adopting children or becoming foster parents, and LGBT people teaching in primary and secondary schools. State-sanctioned, organized hostility to LGBT families has been particularly strong since the 1950s, when lesbians and gay men began forming political groups to fight for equality under the law. Lesbians were (and still are) more likely than gay men to have families that include children. This is because women often came out after they had been married and were frequently denied, or had to fight for, custody of the children from their marriage. For these families, and for the growing lesbian movement more broadly, questions of lesbian parenting became a matter of great importance. In 1956, the San Francisco–based Daughters of Bilitis sponsored discussions titled "Raising Children in a Deviant Relationship." They quickly questioned the word "deviant" by placing it in quotes when they later reported on the event in their magazine, the *Ladder*. For its two decades of publication, the *Ladder* was filled with stories of lesbians dealing with the legal system as they tried to keep their children.[1]

This discrimination has continued far after the LGBT rights movement gained substantial ground on many other issues. In 1985, Massachusetts, a relatively liberal state, reacted to complaints that a gay couple, Don Babets and David Jean, were raising two foster children by revising the state foster care policy to exclude homosexual parents. The change was spearheaded by liberal Democratic governor, and presidential hopeful, Michael Dukakis. Thanks to a four-year court battle waged by Boston-based Gay and Lesbian Advocates and Defenders, the policy was eventually overturned.

In 1993, a Virginia court took Sharon Bottoms's son away from her and granted custody to her homophobic mother, who had claimed that Bottoms's open lesbianism was a danger to the child. The court ruled that since Bottoms "admitted in this court that she is living in an active homosexual relationship," and since homosexual acts were illegal in Virginia at the time, her "conduct [was] illegal and immoral and renders her unfit to parent."[2] Shockingly, the judge granted custody to Bottoms's mother, despite the fact that Sharon Bottoms had claimed in court that her mother's live-in boyfriend had sexually abused her twice a week when she was a teenager. Sharon Bottoms won on appeal, but lost her child again when her mother re-appealed the case.

In each of these cases—Don Babets and David Jean in "liberal" Massachusetts, Sharon Bottoms in "conservative" Virginia—lesbian and gay parents were not assessed for the quality of their parenting care nor how they related to their children. They were judged, and found lacking, on the basis of pernicious stereotypes about homosexuality. A primary example of this is the idea that many LGBT people are child molesters or pedophiles. While this idea is most often associated with gay men, it is also used against lesbians, as well as bisexual and transgender people. The labeling of LGBT people, particularly gay men, as child molesters had its first fever pitch in the 1930s, when J. Edgar Hoover penned a series of newspaper op-ed pieces warning Americans about the new danger to the American child and the American family—the "sexual psychopath" or the "sex criminal." While never explicitly mentioning homosexuality, Hoover's coded subtext made it clear that this new, lurking "monster" was the single adult male who was sexually driven to molest children and thus gay (see myth 4, "Sexual Abuse Causes Homosexuality").[3]

Hoover's paranoiac scenario emerged from very concrete

historical precedents. Since the Middle Ages, groups of people who were considered outsiders by mainstream society were often accused of harming children. This accusation served to demonize and criminalize outsiders. Jews, for instance, were accused of murdering, and sometimes sexually abusing, Christian infants and children in religious rituals. This primal anti-Semitic myth was also used by the Third Reich against European Jews during the Holocaust. In sixteenth-century Japan, European Jesuit missionaries were accused of molesting children. Chinese male immigrants in nineteenth-century California were accused of sexually assaulting young white girls.

Worry over the corruptibility of children has exaggerated and reinforced the idea of childhood innocence and, in particular, childhood itself as utterly innocent of sexuality and sexual knowledge (see myth 16, "There's No Such Thing as a Gay or Trans Child"). Beneath the myth that LGBT parents are bad for children lies the fear that exposure to the wrong sorts of sexual identity ruins any child's supposed innocence. This fear keeps the focus on categorizing the right or wrong kinds of parents rather than on the relations between children and parents.

In the 1920s, LGBT people were becoming increasingly visible in US popular culture. They became identified as a clearly defined group, and groups don't raise children; they aren't families. Ironically, this group identity emerged from the fact that they had been stigmatized. Yet this stigmatization became the reason to view them as an ever-increasing threat. The demonization of LGBT people as bad for children is a continuation of a clear historical pattern of demonizing an entire group by accusing it of child predation.

To a large degree, the monstrous homosexual pervert is at the heart of the myth that LGBT parents are bad for children, maybe especially, their own. Most heterosexual Americans would probably agree that the notion that LGBT parents are active child molesters is patently absurd. They also would not want to see themselves as prejudiced against LGBT people. Nonetheless, a significant percentage of Americans—29 percent, according to a 2009 Gallup poll—still believe lesbian and gay men should not be elementary school teachers. Prejudice and discrimination are far more often expressed not in the form of the big, obviously egregious lies, but in tamer, more nuanced, less obviously discriminatory ones. Often, these more socially acceptable prejudices are not even understood by the people who hold them as exhibiting prejudice. They experience their views and themselves as reasonable or tolerant.

In contemporary society, these socially acceptable prejudices are often cloaked in vague, unproven, pseudoscientific psychological and sociological language and arguments. Experts speak about the "less than ideal" conditions for raising children, or introduce innuendos about "the child's best interests."

This myth's power also emerges from the argument that children are the natural, biological result of the sexual activity between a man and a woman. Because pregnancy cannot result from the sexual union of two women or two men, it is therefore unnatural for non-heterosexual people to have or raise children. This biological argument makes no sense. It presumes that women and men have sex primarily for the sake of reproduction and not pleasure. It ignores the reality that pregnancy resulting from heterosexual sex is often completely unintended, with neither parent wanting the child. It ignores the science and technology that make pregnancy possible through nontraditional means such as alternative insemination, in-vitro fertilization, egg transplants, and embryo transfers. While lesbians, gay men, and transgender people may use some of these technologies to have children, they are overwhelmingly used by heterosexuals.

The argument also discounts the fact that single people and couples, both heterosexual and homosexual, form families through adoption and surrogacy. If female-male sexual intercourse is the only biologically and morally natural method for creating children, then two conclusions follow. First, heterosexuals who require the assistance of reproductive technologies in order to conceive a child are unnatural parents. Second, those heterosexuals who do conceive children "naturally" through male-female intercourse are biologically destined to be good parents. We know neither of these is the case. Good parenting is a form of care based in an ongoing social tie; it is not a biological given.

Promoting the reproductive heterosexual couple as the gold standard for making families furthers the argument that children need two parents of the "opposite sex," a mother and father, so that they will grow up to be gender-appropriate, heterosexual adults. One popular psychological and sociological argument against gay men and lesbians parenting is that children are harmed because they are not provided with "correct" gender or sexual role models. This places the children at risk by making it difficult for them to develop stable, heterosexual, and gender-typical identities. The argument that children of gay or lesbian parents are more likely to become gay, or to have disturbed gender identities, is used in child-custody and same-sex-marriage cases. There is no evidence that children of gay or lesbian parents are more likely to be gay. But even if it were true, why would this be a problem if you believe there is nothing wrong with growing up to be gay, lesbian, bisexual, or transgender?[4]

Studies aside, common sense tells us that the same-sex or different-sex attractions of parents have little to do with those attractions in their children. Almost all LGBT people were born to heterosexual parents. The fear that children of same-sex parents are deprived because their parents are of the same gender—thus denying them the shaping influence of a parent of the "opposite sex"—is, on the face of it, absurd. Children have so many influences in their lives—extended family, families of friends, schools, the media—that the idea they have no exposure to "opposite sex" role models is simply untrue.

All these arguments against LGBT parents are facile, false, and beside the point. The reality is that LGBT adults have for many years created families that are dynamic and highly functional. The 2010 census concluded that about 25 percent of self-identified lesbian or gay households were raising children. Lesbians and gay men have done this despite receiving little to no social support outside of their communities and despite being penalized by the American judicial and legislative systems, as well as by public and private social service agencies.

Overwhelmingly, peer-reviewed studies show that children in single- or two-parent lesbian or gay households grow up no different from children in similar single- or two-parent heterosexual households. For example, twenty-one peer-reviewed psychological studies of lesbian-headed families, published between 1981 and 1998, all found the difference between lesbian parenting and heterosexual parenting negligible.

In 2002, the American Academy of Pediatrics reported that:

A growing body of scientific literature demonstrates that children who grow up with 1 or 2 gay and/or lesbian parents fare as well in emotional, cognitive, social, and sexual functioning as do children whose parents are heterosexual. Children's optimal development seems to be influenced more by the nature of the relationships and interactions within the family unit than by the particular structural form it takes.

These studies are important not only because they debunk the myth that LGBT parents are harmful to children. They also offer the basis for legal arguments that can lead to changes that may be helpful for LGBT families. In 2004, the American Psychiatric Association formally opposed all "legislation proposed at the federal and state levels that would amend the US Constitution or state constitutions, respectively, to prohibit marriage between same-sex couples." There are many other instances—such as issues of adoption, custody, and access to fertility technology and social services—in which these studies may help establish legal and policy precedent that will help same-sex couples create, and sustain, families.

The lived expertise on this question is not found in psychology departments and research centers. Religious and social conservatives who make the argument that gay parents harm their children never ask the real experts on this topic: the children of lesbian and gay parents. In the past decade, children raised in LGBT households have been organizing on their own behalf. COLAGE: People with a Lesbian, Gay, Bisexual, Transgender, or Queer Parent, is a national group whose members speak out about their experience and support other LGBT families. As a result, the children of LGBT parents are being heard more frequently. Zach Wahls, author of *My Two Moms: Lessons of Love, Strength, and What Makes a Family*, spoke to great applause at the 2012 Democratic National Convention as he supported marriage equality.

The often bitter debate that swirls around LGBT families cloaks the larger discussion: how do we all create a culture that nurtures all children, in all kinds of families, to grow into happy, loving, successful adults? It would be as foolish to argue that LGBT parents are all great parents as it would be to argue that they are intrinsically bad parents. We live in a society that, in many ways, does not respect children as full human beings and treats them as helpless for far longer than is realistic. As a result, our society places enormous, unreasonable expectations on parents. Until we create new ways for parents and children to live healthily together, neither will grow and thrive, especially as families.

MYTH 9

SAME-SEX MARRIAGE HARMS TRADITIONAL MARRIAGE

Over the past decade, US attitudes toward same-sex marriage have changed dramatically. A 2004 poll conducted by the nonpartisan Pew Forum on Religion and Public Life found that 31 percent of Americans supported same-sex marriage, while 60 percent were opposed. In contrast, a 2012 Pew poll showed that 48 percent of respondents favored legal recognition of lesbian and gay marriages, and 43 percent opposed it. These same numbers are reflected in other national polls taken in 2012. A CBS News poll conducted shortly after the November 2012 elections found that 51 percent of respondents said same-sex marriage should be legal, 41 percent were opposed, and 8 percent were undecided or had no opinion. Despite this general shift in favor of same-sex marriage, the issue remains deeply polarizing. With the 2013 Supreme Court decision allowing same-sex married couples access to federal benefits, we have seen polling numbers show even more acceptance of marriage equality.

People's opinions about marriage tell us a great deal about what we, as individuals and as a society, value morally, culturally, and materially. Marriage is also a deeply personal matter. It does not mean the same thing to all people. Not everyone wants to get married. Moreover, being married does not even mean the same thing, day to day, year to year, for any two people. Some people's marriages end in divorce. Other marriages flourish. Others may fluctuate among periods of happiness, boredom, certainty, unhappiness, rediscovered bliss, and ambivalence. This is true for heterosexual as well as gay and lesbian married couples. No doubt, similar experiences occur in the many other ways people make intimate and abiding commitments.

Marriage, as a social institution in the United States, has changed over the centuries. We have seen this dramatically over the past four decades. The term "traditional marriage" can't possibly encompass all the ways marriage exists in our culture, let alone all the intimate, everyday ways people experience it.

Nonetheless, one of the most persistent and rhetorically persuasive arguments against legal recognition of same-sex marriage is that it harms "traditional marriage" and the "traditional family." In October 2012, former senator and former Republican presidential hopeful Rick Santorum addressed a fund-raiser for the Family Policy Institute of Washington, a group opposed to same-sex marriage. He spoke in favor of repealing a recently passed law legalizing same-sex marriage in the state of Washington. Senator Santorum decried the "normalization" of gay marriage and homosexuality; unless we win this fight, he warned, "not only will the family disintegrate—it is disintegrating." The majority of voters in Washington State ignored Santorum's warnings, and voted to affirm marriage equality.

Senator Santorum's language was extreme, but his views are shared by many people, and not only by conservatives. The Defense of Marriage Act (DOMA), which defines marriage as the union of one man and one woman and bans any federal recognition of same-sex marriage, was passed with large bipartisan majorities in both the House and Senate and signed into law by President Bill Clinton, a Democrat, in 1996. In 2011, the administration of Democratic president Barack Obama announced its desire to repeal DOMA. Nevertheless, the idea that marriage equality imperils "traditional marriage" feels true to many people. This is evident in the name of the law: the Defense of Marriage Act. And the hard reality is that one out of four Americans remains opposed to same-sex marriage.

What do people think they are defending when they defend "traditional marriage"? Are they, like Santorum, worried about its disintegration? Ironically, Santorum is right about one thing: disintegration is already underway. Well before gay marriage became a political demand, or a legal reality, marriage and the family were in the midst of seismic upheavals. Divorce rates have been skyrocketing, single-parent households are increasing, blended families of all sorts are now the norm, and the stay-at-home mom is a dwindling reality for many children. The movement for same-sex marriage did not cause these changes. In many ways, it is a product of these same cultural forces—especially feminism—that have remade gender roles and allowed women to enter the paid work force. Many women entered the paid workforce out of desire, but many did so because they—and their families—had no other option. Economic forces, such as declining real wages and the erosion of job security for so many workers, pose real threats to "traditional families."

Many people are deeply uncomfortable with these changes and irrationally blame them on LGBT people in general and same-sex marriage in particular. LGBT people thus become scapegoats for a wider set of social transformations. We see this not just in debates over same-sex marriage, but in moral panics about endangered children and predatory homosexuals (see myth 8, "LGBT Parents Are Bad for Children").

Extreme opposition to same-sex marriage often is framed in apocalyptic terms, as if two brides or two grooms will end civilization as we know it. Such worries are logically absurd, but fear is not about logic.

Can same-sex marriage somehow cause the end of civilization, and even the human race? There is no evidence for this worry. Heterosexuals who choose to will still get married and have children. Some will have children without getting married. The ability to marry a same-sex partner will not lure wavering or curious heterosexuals to "go gay"—with disastrous consequences for the repopulation of the human species. Homosexuality is not a lifestyle choice that people opt into or out of depending on what is trending. In US states where same-sex marriage has been legalized, there has been a decrease in neither heterosexual marriage rates nor in birth rates. The example of Massachusetts—the first state to legalize same-sex marriage—is telling. Data show that in the years since same-sex couples could legally marry in Massachusetts, starting in 2004, the state's marriage rate has remained stable, and its divorce rate has actually gone down.[1]

In a 2004 essay, "The End of Marriage in Scandinavia: The 'Conservative Case' for Same-Sex Marriage Collapses," conservative commentator Stanley Kurtz made a provocative argument that same-sex marriage spells the end of heterosexual marriage.[2] Kurtz argued that same-sex marriage had caused the decline of heterosexual marriage in Denmark, Norway, and Sweden, all of which had given marital rights to same-sex couples. The data do not support his argument. Economist M. V. Lee Badgett points out that heterosexual marriage rates in all three countries went up in the years since they first approved registered partnerships for same-sex couples: Denmark, in 1989; Norway, in 1993; and Sweden, in 1994. Same-sex marriage has since been legalized in all three countries, still with no decline in heterosexual marriage.[3]

Does this mean same-sex marriage is good for "opposite-sex" marriage? Maybe, but maybe not. Just because two phenomena appear in rough succession does not mean one caused the other, especially with so complex and multifactorial an issue as marriage.

Some progressive advocates of marriage equality have suggested that same-sex marriage might change marriage for the better by promoting gender equality between men and women in heterosexual marriages. By modeling egalitarian partnering, same-sex couples may help break down the traditional gender roles that have historically caused social and economic discrepancies between men and women. This could make for happier heterosexual couples.

In this way, same-sex marriage potentially helps expand what is possible for all marriages and does so from within the institution of marriage. Progressive proponents of marriage equality are not mocking marriage, but are recognizing that how two people make an intimate life need not be dictated by past forms of marriage. Marriage always has served multiple purposes, and will continue to do so.

The conservative media blitz over the alleged "end of marriage" simply ignores the many realities of how people make intimate commitments and form families. All societies need, and are obliged to provide, multiple, usually overlapping, structures to support the people who live in them, including those who live together in familial groups. That's what makes these social supports and living arrangements traditions. The composition of familial groups varies from culture to culture. Because societies change over time, so too must the forms any society relies on to provide stability and security for its members. But this is also why "traditional marriage" has never actually existed; there has never been only one living arrangement that can support human intimacies or families. Humans have imagined and created a wide array of social and familial forms for arranging their lives.

The "traditional" grouping of husband, wife, and children is the arrangement put forth by conservatives as the most statistically common—even though it is not now and likely never was. It is also touted as the best. However, we see so many different familial forms in our lives and in our neighborhoods. These include multiple generations of one family living together and supporting one another economically and emotionally, or best friends raising kids together. And what about an unmarried couple raising children together? These are common to every community. Or think about three unrelated adults, who may or may not be sexually intimate, pledging to look after each other in sickness and health. All of these relationships, along with marriage, are productive and valuable social structures that support and sustain relationships and life.

Opponents of same-sex marriage refuse to recognize the wonderful human ability to build and maintain many forms of family life. For example, the Maine anti-marriage-equality organization Maine4Marriage has stated, "For millennia and across all cultures, traditional man/woman marriage has been the essential foundation of all successful societies." This is simply not true. The "traditional family"—romantic heterosexual couple with children—is a recent invention. Historians such as Nancy Cott, John D'Emilio, and Estelle Freedman have shown that heterosexual marriage has taken different forms, meant different things in various cultures, and fulfilled very different social functions.

What do advocates of "traditional marriage" mean when they refer to the timeless values of man/woman marriage? Is it the traditional principle of couverture, which we find in English common law (the backbone of colonial and contemporary American law), in which a man and woman became one legal person upon marriage? In practice, this legal and social unity of the couple meant that the woman ceased to exist as a legal identity with her own rights. A husband could sell his wife's property without her consent, and had the legal ability—even duty—to make all decisions for them both. The tradition of couverture existed well into the nineteenth century in the United States.

Do advocates of "traditional marriage" want to defend the version of marriage in which a man could legally rape his wife? Nineteenth-century feminists in the United States campaigned vigorously to eliminate the spousal exemption for rape. Sadly, it took several generations of activism to force the change. North Carolina became the last state to criminalize marital rape—in 1993.

Perhaps defenders of "traditional marriage" want to go back to a time when states legally—through antimiscegenation laws—forbade interracial heterosexual couples from marrying? Such laws were finally held to be unconstitutional by the Supreme Court in *Loving v. Virginia*, in 1967.

Marriage is a civil institution organized by the state, and structured by rules and regulations. It establishes a next-of-kin relationship between spouses and puts into place a series of interlocking legal rights and responsibilities. Among them, married couples can: reduce tax liability by filing a joint return; receive special government benefits, such as those given to surviving spouses and dependents under Social Security provisions; inherit from each other even when no will has been made; retain custody of children upon the death of the other parent; refuse to testify against a spouse in a court of law; and easily gain US residency for a foreign-born spouse.

There are also a large number of social benefits granted through marriage. These benefits may include: access to the health-care plans of a spouse, if he or she is lucky enough to have employer-provided health insurance; hospital and prison visitation; family memberships to places such as gyms and museums, as well as family discounts on other purchases; and tenancy succession.

Many of these legal and social privileges can be gained through making individual legal contracts. Same-sex couples and unmarried heterosexual couples (as well as people in other types of relationships) can draw up wills, establish guardianship provisions, and name their partner as health-care proxy. There are, however, no guarantees these contracts will always be respected, especially if the legally recognized family members of an LGB person contest a will or custody arrangement. Such piecemeal contracting is also exhausting, expensive, and often not realistically available to people who cannot afford to hire lawyers. And many of these rights—especially in such areas as immigration and federal income tax—are granted only through marriage.

Civil marriage—and only civil marriage—grants couples more than 1,200 federal and state benefits. It also—whether we agree that this is a good thing or not—gives married people a special, elevated social status. To paraphrase Nancy Cott, there is nothing like marriage, except marriage.[4] As a matter of basic fairness and equality, if marriage is the only way to access these benefits, then same-sex couples deserve equal access to the institution of civil marriage.

Of course, no one wants to get married just to receive these material benefits. People usually get married because they fall in love, want to spend their lives together, possibly raise a family. However, we live in a world of economic realities, and these benefits are essential to individuals' and couples' well-being. For many people, marriage is the only way to get access to health care and government benefits, such as spousal Social Security, or to secure a legal relationship with their children. Not only does same-sex marriage not harm traditional marriage, but a strong moral and legal argument can be made that the denial of marriage equality harms LGB people. The movement for marriage equality is, in many ways, a testament to the enduring emotional, symbolic, and material value of marriage and family life—and to a profoundly American ideal of fairness.

Do all LGBT people think same-sex marriage is a positive, progressive move into the future? Probably all of them agree that, if civil marriage is available to heterosexuals, it should be available to same-sex couples on equal terms. However, some feminist and LGBT critics of same-sex marriage argue that the way certain public benefits are built into civil marriage impedes making social changes that could benefit everybody. Why, they ask, should access to health care be connected to marital status at all? They worry that the same-sex-marriage movement is settling for too little. It will do nothing for those many people—LGBT and straight—who do not want to marry but who do need health insurance or equal access to citizenship. Nor does civil marriage for same-sex couples reflect the diverse and imaginative ways LGBT people make kinship ties.

If same-sex marriage were available in all fifty states, would all LGB people want to get married? Of course not. Not all heterosexual people want to get married. In recent decades, heterosexuals have been getting married later and later in life, and many prefer to live together outside marriage. In the short time and in the few states that same-sex marriage has been legal, an interesting gendered difference has emerged: lesbian couples are marrying at far greater rates than gay male couples, by a ratio of 2 to 1 in Massachusetts, for example.[5] Is this because women are socialized to settle down and men are encouraged to play the field? Or are other factors in play, such as the greater likelihood that lesbian couples have children and, thus, have more need of the kinds of protections legal marriage offers?

Will younger lesbians and gay men want to marry? We have no way of knowing this. However, women and men born in the past thirty years have grown up in a very different world from previous generations. Marriage for them is not the standard that it was in the 1950s or 1960s. They may not have the same romantic notions of marriage that older lesbians and gay men might. For younger gay men and lesbians, then, marriage may simply be one of many options. On the other hand, as beneficiaries of earlier feminist challenges to make marriage more equal, younger gay men and lesbians may find that marriage now fits their political views and intimate desires.

The reality is that marriage remains a powerful cultural ideal, which we are all taught to value. Advocates of same-sex marriage do not advocate destroying marriage, or abandoning it; they embrace it. Will same-sex marriage change how we—as a society—think about marriage? Yes, of course. And that's more than okay. Will lesbians and gay men now feel the same pressure to marry that heterosexuals long have? This would not be okay. It would be a bittersweet victory for marriage equality if success meant simply replicating social hierarchy by stigmatizing people, gay or straight, who choose not to marry and who instead organize their lives around less legally formalized relationships, or even around more-casual encounters.

Marriage has survived any number of changes over the centuries. Legalizing same-sex marriage will not end the institution. It will not even be the end of the fight for sexual freedom and social equality for all people. Nonetheless, marriage equality has the potential to show an ever-widening straight and LGBT public the multiple ways people can love and be for one another.

MYTH 10

ALL RELIGIONS CONDEMN HOMOSEXUALITY

Religions are richly variable in their organizations, belief systems, rituals, and practices. This is true across cultures and history. Grand statements about what "all religions" say or believe about anything—especially about such a complex phenomenon as human desire and sexuality—are not just unhelpful, they're impossible. Nonetheless, this has not prevented many Christian opponents of homosexuality from asserting that all religions condemn homosexuality. This assertion is patently false; it is not even the case that all Christianities condemn homosexuality. The myth that all religions condemn homosexuality passes off one strand of Christian interpretation as a universal moral claim about what "all religions" and "all religious people" believe. In fact, what religions have to say about homosexuality varies considerably not just among religions, but within religions, too.

Religions are internally diverse. Although we are used to referring to Christianity, Hinduism, Judaism, Islam, or Buddhism in the singular, we could more accurately refer to these dynamic ways of organizing human relationships in the plural: as Christianities, Hinduisms, Judaisms, Islams, Buddhisms. This shift from singular to plural may sound odd, but is helpful when it reminds us that no religion is monolithic. What any religion means in the lives of its practitioners changes across historical periods, geographical locations, and in relation to other social forces.

We can see this clearly in the case of Hinduism's complex and changing attitudes toward homosexuality. Same-sex attachments and desire were both known and generally tolerated in ancient and medieval India, as reflected in such sacred texts as the Kama Sutra and Krittivasa Ramayana. It was not until India came under British colonial rule—with its Christian assumptions about sex—that Section 377, the first Indian law banning "carnal intercourse against the order of nature," was passed, in 1860.[1] The efforts of modern-day Indian activists—both Hindu and non-Hindu—for sexual rights finally led to the overturning of Section 377, in 2009.

A religion is not practiced in a vacuum. It lives and breathes through individuals and the communities they build in particular times and places. This living, breathing religion does not stand apart from larger political struggles, but is embedded in them in complicated ways, as the above history of Hinduism and homosexuality shows.

Value judgments—what we might also call morality—are not monopolized by religion. You do not have to be religious to live morally. All people are capable of making value judgments and acting in relation to others in accord with deeply held ethical principles—and they do, in big and small ways every day. But in the United States, due to the historical importance of Christian thinking, there is a strong tendency to conflate religion and values. Many Americans believe that the only way to have values and be moral is to be religious, and then, only in a Christian way.[2] This is not how the terms "morality" or "values" are being used here, however.

Buddhism offers an important counter to the usual ways of framing this issue as a matter of the morality of heterosexuality versus the immorality of homosexuality. In both branches of Buddhism, Theravada and Mahayana (which houses both Zen and Tibetan schools), the key distinction is not between good heterosexuality and bad homosexuality, but between celibacy and sexuality. Celibacy is the religious ideal, but Buddhism recognizes that very few people can achieve it. For laypersons, the goal is to avoid sexual misconduct. Buddhist rejections of same-sex desire and sexual activity are relatively rare, but, where they do occur, they must be understood as part of a more general suspicion of any expression of carnal desire. More generally, Buddhist moral appraisal of homosexuality varies with its host cultures. In places that are more accepting of homosexuality and gender variance, same-sex desire is more likely to be seen as a permissible and potentially correct conduct.[3]

When a religion does condemn homosexuality, what is it condemning? Is it same-sex sexual acts and, if so, which ones? Or is it homosexual identity? Or both?

Consider what the Bible has to say about homosexuality. The short answer is: not much. The longer answer requires understanding that sacred texts are given meaning through interpretation; these interpretations change over time and can also vary within any particular period. The Hebrew Bible—what Christians call the Old Testament—does mention and condemn same-sex sexual behavior, but only three times, twice in Leviticus (18:22 and 20:13) and once in Genesis (19:1–11), in the story of Sodom and Gomorrah. In the New Testament, homosexual acts might be mentioned, depending on the interpretation, in Paul's letter to the Romans condemning men's "shameless" sexual acts with each other (just which acts are not named) and in his condemnation of women's "unnatural" sexual acts (1:26–27).[4]

Biblical and Talmudic scholars, as well as historians specializing in the study of premodern Christianity, have convincingly argued that these passages do not condemn homosexuality as we think of it today. The Hebrew Bible and the New Testament had no concept of homosexuality as a personal identity. These few Biblical passages focused on sexual behavior. Scholars have worked hard to determine what these passages and their exact words meant in their day, and for ours. Some of the results are surprising. What are these passages so worried about if it is not the idea of a homosexual person or a personal identity?

Contemporary scholars argue that the moral transgression of Sodom was not male-male sexual relations, but the gross abuse of guests. The men of Sodom came to Lot's door and demanded that he hand over his two male houseguests (angels in disguise) so they could forcibly "know" them. In Biblical language, "know" means to have sex with. So the Sodom story is about the threat of rape and the violation of laws of hospitality to strangers—a very important issue for a nomadic people.

Lot is also an honored figure in Islam's holy book, the Quran, where the story of Lot's people and the destruction of Sodom appears five times.[5] Islamic commentaries from the medieval period show a diversity of scholarly and legal views about the precise "sin" of Sodom, although the interpretation that became dominant identifies it with male-male anal sex. Under Sharia, or Islamic law, same-sex sexual acts were early on condemned, especially anal sex between men. But Islamic jurists have disagreed both historically and today as to what the proper penalty for male homosexual acts should be. Historically, sex between women seems to have attracted far less commentary by either medieval or contemporary jurists, and little in the way of mandated penalties.

In the twentieth century, various Islamic revivalist movements, particularly within Sunni Islam, seeking to be traditional or authentic have tended to call for the death penalty for male homosexual acts. They claim this is the Islamic position. This obscures historical as well as contemporary differences of interpretation within Islam and across very different Muslim-majority countries.[6] Still, the death penalty is on the books (if rarely meted out) as a possible punishment for male homosexuality in several countries, including Iran and Saudi Arabia. In early 2012, a Shiite militia group in Iraq—where homosexuality is not illegal—tortured and murdered more than forty men thought to be homosexual. The murders were denounced by Iraqi human rights groups as well as by international LGBT activists. The Iraqi government did not condemn or even address the murders.

All this may seem shocking, but, sadly, the criminalization and severe legal punishment of homosexuality are hardly unique to countries that follow Islamic law. In contemporary Uganda, legislators influenced by the most conservative versions of evangelical

Christianity, especially versions imported from the United States, have been debating making homosexual sex a capital crime. (Homosexual acts are already against the law in Uganda.) And Russia's government, looking to shore up its popularity, increasingly embraces the antigay theology of the Russian Orthodox Church by cracking down on LGBT people, especially activists.

In recent years, the interpretation of the story of Sodom and Gomorrah as a condemnation of rape and inhospitality has been taken up by contemporary LGBT Muslim groups, such as Toronto-based Salaam and US-based Al-Fatiha, and by a growing number of Muslim scholars in order to push back against the most conservative Islamic voices and open a space for Muslim gender and sexual minorities. The Internet also provides a vital resource for LGBT Muslims seeking to develop and put forward their own religious perspectives about same-sex desires and identities.[7]

Where Leviticus is concerned, only anal sex between men is explicitly condemned. Notably, the Hebrew Bible is completely silent on the question of lesbianism. Talmudic scholar Daniel Boyarin suggests that Leviticus's prohibition on male-male anal intercourse actually concerns a "mixing of kinds."[8] A man who lets himself be penetrated by another man takes the subordinate position assigned to women. In so doing, he violates rules of manhood, "mixing" or confusing his proper status. Leviticus's prohibition, then, like the story of Sodom, warns against the transgression of social codes that ensure an ordered society. Being penetrated by another man, or raping two male houseguests, is a metaphor for disorder and the neglect of social constraint. Such a scenario may seem extreme for the lesson it imparts, but that is how allegories teach us moral lessons.

Historically, the most frequently cited scriptural passages in all three Abrahamic traditions—Judaism, Christianity, and Islam—provide little convincing evidence to justify legal or social discrimination against LGBT people. What the Bible does or does not really say about homosexuality is less the point than how living, breathing historical people organize meanings and judgments around sexual activity and how we think about our bodies.

What of Christianity, the dominant religion in the United States? A large majority of Americans identify as Christian, and even non-Christians may find themselves holding "Christian" ideas about sex and proper and improper uses of the body. Additionally, whether you are Christian or not, in the United States you will be subject to laws that are directly influenced by Christianity's historical ambivalence about, and even fear of, the body and sex. A dominant line of Christian theology has identified the "lusts of the flesh" with human fallenness—sometimes called "original sin"— and seen sex and the body as places where humans are especially liable to exhibit possessiveness, greed, and corruption. A lesser tradition within Christian theology seeks to affirm the body. In the United States, Christian ambivalence toward sexuality and the body has been handed down through Protestant theology. Elsewhere in the Americas, and in much of continental Europe, there is a similar, but specifically Catholic theology surrounding the body and sexuality.

Whether affirming or warning against sex, moral teaching is as much about prescriptions for how to live peacefully and productively with others as it is about prohibitions. These principles are often informed by and learned through religious morality. But you do not have to be religious to agree that treating your neighbor with respect and dignity is a good thing. The very concept of separation of church and state reinforces the idea that moral rules and ethical practices do not have to be tied to religion at all. These common principles do not require that we all agree. They are the social context in which we can peacefully disagree and morally engage with one another despite our many differences (see myth 11, "Gay Rights Infringe on Religious Liberty").

In public discussions of homosexuality and same-sex marriage, many self-identified religious people openly disagree with the official positions of their religious leaders. For example, a strong majority of lay Catholics support antidiscrimination laws and even same-sex marriage or civil unions. A March 2011 report by the Public Religion Research Institute found that "nearly three-quarters of Catholics favor either allowing gay and lesbian people to marry (43%) or allowing them to form civil unions (31%). Only 22% of Catholics say there should be no legal recognition of a gay couple's relationship." A growing number of mainline Protestants and evangelicals also support some form of legal recognition of same-sex relationships. This is especially true for Christians between the ages of eighteen and thirty-four. There is often a wide gap between the pronouncements of religious leaders and the values held by individuals who have, in their own conscience, and in the context of shared social life, made their own decisions about the morality of homosexuality.

Some religious traditions openly welcome LGBT members and will sanctify same-sex unions. There is even an evangelical Christian ministry dedicated primarily to LGBT people, the Metropolitan Community Church, founded in 1968 by Reverend Troy Perry. (Perry, originally a Pentecostal minister, was defrocked for his homosexuality.) Nevertheless, the public debate over LGBT rights and same-sex marriage has overwhelmingly pitted religious values against civil equality. This ignores the reality that equality is also a moral—and, for many, a religious—value. This polarizing debate leaves out the great diversity of perspectives many religious people hold on same-sex marriage and other issues regarding sexual behavior. Just because you're religious does not mean you are against either homosexuality or same-sex marriage on religious grounds. Again, you might support it on religious grounds.'

Two mainline Protestant denominations recognize and perform same-sex marriages: the United Church of Christ and Unitarian Universalists. Several others—the Presbyterian Church (USA), the Evangelical Lutheran Church in America, and, most recently, the Episcopal Church—allow individual congregations to support and bless same-sex unions. Within Judaism, both the Reform and Reconstructionist Jewish movements support same-sex marriage and permit individual rabbis to officiate at same-sex weddings. The Conservative movement also allows individual rabbis to bless same-sex unions, but has so far stopped short of endorsing same-sex marriage.

Despite this great diversity of religious attitudes toward homosexuality and same-sex marriage, many people believe that debates over religion and sexuality irrevocably mean taking one of two opposed sides. Some people argue that sexuality must be limited, or controlled, by morality—in the form of religion—for the good of an ordered society. Others counter that sexuality needs to be freed from the repressive constraints of religion.

Ironically, both opponents and supporters of LGBT equality believe in this supposedly uncrossable divide between religion and sexuality. Versions of this argument are so frequently repeated by media commentators, politicians, and activists that they have become common sense. This is not just about homosexuality. In reporting on a range of issues related to sexual life—such as birth control, "out-of-wedlock" births, abortion, and even sexual assault—the US media overwhelmingly quote the most conservative religious perspectives as the moral position on an issue. This means that conservative Christians, usually evangelical or Catholic, get the most airtime. Is it any wonder, then, that many LGBT people and feminists identify religion as "the enemy"?

Blanket proclamations such as "religion is the enemy" overlook the many self-identified feminists and LGBT people who are religious and who do not think they should have to choose between their sexuality and their religion. For these LGBT people and their allies, it would be simplistic, and arrogant, to condemn religion as "the enemy." This equation implies that all religions and all religious people are universally hostile to homosexuality. This is exactly what religious conservatives want us to believe: that all religions condemn homosexuality.

This false choice misses another major point. Respect between people of different sexualities, and even within individual relationships, can make sexuality and desire productive forces in society. Sexual intimacies are a form of human relating. They often are the basis for creating moral ways to imagine and make lives with other people. This does not mean that every time you have sex, you have a moral breakthrough. It does mean that sex has the capacity to help us forge deep ties and knit larger communities, a primary purpose of many religions.[10] An example of this is how, in the early years of the AIDS crisis in the 1980s, gay men were able to come together to confront the crisis when the US government did not. By drawing on already-developed sexual networks and institutions, such as bars and clubs, gay men were able to care for the sick, start educating one another about HIV/AIDS, and save their own lives. Gay men created not just political alliances, but alternate forms of kinship, out of their ways of relating to each other sexually. Lesbians have done this as well.

Religious people continue to struggle within their communities to integrate their understanding of their traditions with the realities of the LGBT people in their midst as neighbors, family members, and fellow congregants. For many religiously active LGBT people and their allies, it may make sense to engage in debates with religious conservatives about how to interpret particular religious texts or implement traditions. Such debates are already taking place within many religious communities.

Both religion and sexuality are ways of living—in the language of the US Constitution, forms of "free exercise"—that are essential to, and even define, personal identities. Ways of living are informed by practices as well as by a sense of an inner life. With religion, the inner life is often called conscience. With sexuality, the inner life is the feeling of desire. In both cases, these are profound, lived experiences that make themselves known through practices. Many people "know" what they believe, and many people "know" what and whom they desire, by enacting these beliefs with others. These experiences and feelings keenly inform how individuals understand their lives and make commitments to others. Sexuality and religion may have a lot more in common than most people imagine. Neither has to be discarded or cast out to make room for the other. They can, in fact, be understood through each other.

MYTH 11

GAY RIGHTS INFRINGE ON RELIGIOUS LIBERTY

The argument that gay rights infringe on religious liberty assumes a fundamental antagonism between religion and homosexuality. This is not true. This myth also misunderstands what religious liberty—also called religious freedom—requires in practice. Religious liberty in the United States means that citizens can hold and express differing beliefs. It also means that they have the freedom to practice those beliefs. Because religious liberty creates room for many diverse moral or ethical perspectives, it would be a fantasy to think that as a nation we could reconcile all of our often-contradictory political differences around religion and sexuality on issues such as the moral status of homosexuality. Such a fantasy gives us an inaccurate picture of what democracy and religious freedom would be. The purpose of democracy is to allow, even foster, disagreement.

Religious freedom—enshrined in the First Amendment to the Constitution—is one of the most important principles of American democracy. Religious freedom in the United States has two components: disestablishment, also called church-state separation, and free exercise. Separation of church and state means that no religious belief can be written into the law. This is the necessary precondition for free exercise, which is also called the freedom to practice. In theory, free exercise gives citizens the right to practice any form of religion, as well as the right not to be religious at all.

In real life, things are more complicated. Christianity is the dominant religion in the United States, and over the centuries religious freedom has most often meant the freedom to be Christian in a particular way. When people argue that gay rights infringe on religious liberty, they invariably mean that civil rights for LGBT people infringe on the free exercise rights of conservative religious opponents of gay rights.

This myth addresses the relationship—at the crux of national and legal arguments—between religious liberty and something called "gay rights." (So far, conservative religious groups have not paid a lot of attention to transgender issues; they no doubt eventually will.) "Gay rights" is a misleading term; it suggests that LGB people are asking for "special rights" or "special protections" rather than equality under the law. This is not true, but it is an argument with deep emotional appeal that feels true to many opponents of LGB equality. Falsely naming equal rights for LGB people "special rights" also helps turn the Christian majority into a persecuted minority (see myth 19, "Antidiscrimination Laws in the United States Protect LGBT People").

The United States Conference of Catholic Bishops echoed this sentiment of a persecuted Christian minority in their 2012 "Fortnight for Freedom" campaign. The bishops were concerned that some laws and public policies—same-sex marriage, adoption rights for gay and lesbian couples, abortion, and contraceptive coverage—infringe on Catholics' rights of conscience. Conservative think tanks, such as the Heritage Foundation and the Becket Fund for Religious Liberty, have also stated that antidiscrimination laws and same-sex marriage pose threats to religious liberty. Religious conservatives and even liberal legal scholars have been cataloguing legal collisions between "gay rights" and "religious liberty." These cases will increase as same-sex marriage gains legal recognition in more states.[1] These conflicts do not affect houses of worship, which are constitutionally protected by church-state separation, but are becoming more common in private businesses (wedding photographers, banquet halls, medical offices), religiously affiliated colleges and universities, and agencies such as private adoption services contracted by the state.

Recently Illinois, Massachusetts, and the District of Columbia ruled that Catholic Charities—in order to comply with antidiscrimination laws—had to give equal consideration to same-sex couples applying to be adoptive or foster parents. This was a major challenge; Catholic Charities of Boston had been offering adoption services for 103 years. Catholic leaders, faced with a choice between violating what they saw as Church teachings about homosexuality and abandoning their religious mission to care for needy children, ceased facilitating any adoptions. This regrettable outcome affected children and the dedicated caseworkers who worked for Catholic Charities (many of whom disagreed with the decision). Do state regulations barring discrimination against qualified lesbian and gay male applicants violate Catholic religious liberty? This very complicated issue presents an example of how social and legal commitments to civil rights can result in painful conflict.[2]

Catholic leaders, opponents of homosexuality, and even some legal scholars argue that Catholic Charities was being unfairly coerced by the state to suspend its religious principles. This would be a clear infringement of free exercise. Framing the issue this way, however, reduces the scope of religious liberty to free exercise only. It ignores the other vitally important component of religious freedom: separation of church and state.

It is important to distinguish between acts carried out by individuals and groups functioning as agents for the secular state, and those acts carried out by private religious or secular organizations. Catholic Charities is a private organization that was licensed by the state—and given public monies—to provide foster care and adoption services. As an agent of the state, it was subject to applicable antidiscrimination ordinances. In Massachusetts, state law bars adoption agencies from discriminating on the basis of "race, religion, cultural heritage, political beliefs, national origin, marital status, sexual orientation or disability."[3]

Catholic Church leaders are free to believe that same-sex couples should not be allowed to adopt. They are free to argue that homosexuality is morally wrong. And they are completely free to engage in their religious mission of serving society's neediest. However, a different picture emerges when we examine both aspects of religious freedom. Once Catholic Charities accepts licensure by the state and receives public monies to carry out the secular service of adoption and foster care placements, it is not permitted to enforce its sectarian viewpoint. That would violate the principle of disestablishment, because the state would be subsidizing a religious viewpoint.

Many conservatives view disestablishment as punitive to religion. They see it as forbidding religion to enter the public sphere. Ironically, the reality is that this separation of church and state profoundly provides the public context within which individuals and organizations can enact religious freedom. This context—the shared space of democratic social life—makes possible the flowering of diverse religious and nonreligious moral perspectives. In a society with multiple religions, one group's religious practice may rub up against another's. It is equally possible that religious freedom may come into conflict with other deeply held societal values, such as equality of treatment under the law. These conflicts may not have easy resolutions. If they end up in court, where one side wins and the other loses, the complexity of justice and fair treatment will be lost in the zero-sum battle of winner takes all.

Some legal scholars and policy experts have identified a "competition in rights" between LGB people seeking equality under the law and religious opponents of homosexual behavior. They believe that basic fairness requires some sort of legal "trade-off" or compromise—commonly called conscience clauses or religious exemptions—that would balance competing rights. Catholic Charities did seek a religious exemption before closing its adoption agencies. But—and this is important—it asked for this only where sexual orientation was concerned. In each instance, the state said no.

Despite these setbacks, proponents of religious exemptions have in fact been successful in shaping both public debates and public policies over "at-risk" religious liberty. As a result, there is currently great momentum for building a wide range of religious exemptions into same-sex marriage laws and LGBT civil rights laws. These debates and policy "solutions" are not new. A similar legal trade-off has been argued for—and actively endorsed by state legislatures, Congress, and federal agencies—to "balance" a woman's constitutionally protected right to abortion against a healthcare worker's right to refuse to provide medical services that violate their conscience. Framing this quest for fairness as a matter of intractable divides and required trade-offs poses religious freedom and sexual freedom as intractable antagonists. This is a problem for social equality. It is also not true (see myth 10, "All Religions Condemn Homosexuality").

Conscience clauses are fairly recent. The first federal conscience clause, the Church Amendment of 1973, was passed the same year that *Roe v. Wade* legalized abortions nationwide, and specifically focused on sterilization and abortion. By 1978, virtually every state had adopted some version of a conscience clause for health-care providers who objected to offering certain services on religious or moral grounds.

In debates over LGBT civil rights, religious exemptions have been written into state antidiscrimination statutes. They also are present in the yet-to-be passed, federal Employment Non-Discrimination Act. As written, the bill would prohibit employment discrimination on the basis of sexual orientation or gender identity, but includes an exemption for religious corporations, associations, educational institutions, or societies (see myth 19, "Antidiscrimination Laws in the United States Protect LGBT People").

There are both narrower and broader versions of religious exemptions. The versions in force in the antidiscrimination laws in Massachusetts, Illinois, and Washington, DC, apply to religious organizations, but not to religiously affiliated organizations, privately owned businesses, or individuals. Conservative policy organizations are actively composing a much broader wish list of religious exemptions. They claim these are necessary to avoid the inevitable

burdens antidiscrimination laws and same-sex marriage allegedly
will impose on the religious freedom of groups and individuals
who oppose homosexual behavior and "gay rights." In 2012, when
the Maryland legislature was debating a same-sex-marriage bill, a
group of conservative legal scholars urged "exemptions that would
have permitted individuals and small businesses, as well as religious organizations, to refuse to provide goods, services or benefits
to facilitate or perpetuate any marriage if doing so would 'violate
their sincerely held religious beliefs.'"[4] The Maryland General Assembly declined their advice. However, other state legislatures,
such as New Hampshire's, New York's, and Connecticut's, have enacted various forms of conscience clauses.

There are many problems with placing broad religious exemptions into LGBT antidiscrimination laws. Lawsuits are inevitable.
These will place courts in the complicated position of distinguishing between a sincerely held religious belief, and an unreflective
squeamishness or casual prejudice.[5] Religious belief and social
prejudice are not the same. They do, however, often reinforce each
other. In addition, these broad religious exemptions from applicable civil rights laws may not be constitutional. Many legal scholars
argue that privileging religious motives over other reasons for acting in particular ways constitutes a tacit endorsement of religion,
in violation of the principle of disestablishment. Finally, these exemptions are not only unfair, they essentially do an end run around
the thorny but necessary business of living side by side with people
whose moral views and life practices are different from our own.

No religious group should be required to bless or sanctify a
same-sex marriage if homosexuality is contrary to its values. This
is a simple matter of religious liberty. The state should not, and
constitutionally cannot, impose its own sexual orthodoxy on a religious community. However, this is very different from whether a
religious organization should be permitted to discriminate against
LGBT employees in providing secular benefits, such as health care
or equal access to residential housing, benefits that often come
through employment or through enrollment in a university.

There are parallels here with an earlier US history of racial discrimination, particularly when biblical justifications were offered for slavery and, later, for a complex legal framework of racial discrimination. Some organizations have even argued for religious exemptions for racial discrimination. The most famous example involved Bob Jones University, a private fundamentalist Christian school that, beginning in the 1950s, banned interracial dating and threatened students who disobeyed with expulsion. The university's policy eventually came into conflict with both changing social norms about racial equality and with new state and federal laws banning racial discrimination. Nonetheless, Bob Jones refused to change its interracial dating ban on the grounds that it was a religious tenet. After the IRS removed the university's tax-exempt status, the school sued. The controversy reached the Supreme Court in the 1983 case *Bob Jones v. US.* An 8–1 majority upheld the removal of tax-exempt status, arguing that the government's interest in "eradicating racial discrimination in education . . . substantially outweighs whatever burden denial of tax benefits places on [the University's] exercise of their religious beliefs."[6] The court concluded that religious beliefs are not a blank check for racially discriminatory treatment.

Yet, state and federal courts, as well as legislatures, continue to exempt religious bodies from laws that deal with gender- and sexuality-based discrimination. Legal scholar Martha Minow observes, "The struggles over exemptions from civil rights laws [around race] for religious groups reflect historic political battles, inspired but not dictated by ideals and hammered out through shifts in power from popular mobilization and changes of heart."[7] The Bob Jones decision thus reflected a much longer history of social and legal activism. This activism so profoundly transformed public attitudes about racial discrimination that religious objectors to racial equality were granted almost no credence.

Minow believes that social transformations outside the courts will influence courts to find that religious exemptions in cases of gender-based or sexuality rights are as constitutionally impermissible as racial discrimination. We are not there yet. Legal commentators from across the political spectrum suggest that religious accommodations are required, in the meantime, to guard against backlash. It is clear that we do need arguments and activism outside the narrow parameters of the law. Nevertheless, legal and policy arguments over the need to "balance" religious liberty and LGBT equality ignore that LGBT rights are a matter of religious freedom, too. This is all the more reason vigorously and expansively to debate these issues.

Religious freedom, far from being the opposite of "gay rights," forms a necessary ground for LGBT equality and freedom. How people arrange their intimate relations and their gender identities involves important moral decision-making. This is quite different from a moral consensus, where a mythical "we" have to agree on the acceptable ways very personal sexual and gender choices get lived. As a society, we should be expanding possibilities for religious liberty. We can do this by broadening the scope of what counts as the good life and who counts as worthy of flourishing. In doing this, a context may emerge for changes of heart about what it means to live in a democracy and bump up against people different from ourselves.

MYTH 12

PEOPLE OF COLOR ARE MORE HOMOPHOBIC THAN WHITE PEOPLE

A clear, recent example of the myth that people of color are more homophobic than white people is the discussion of voter turnout for California's Proposition 8, in November 2008. Proposition 8 was a ballot initiative amending the state's constitution to read, "Only marriage between a man and a woman is valid or recognized in California." The amendment essentially overturned the state Supreme Court ruling earlier that year that had allowed same-sex marriage. Both proponents and opponents raised enormous amounts of money, and lobbying for and against the ballot initiative was fierce, often focusing on bringing specific communities to the polls. The final vote was 52.24 percent for Prop 8 and 47.76 percent against. In the analysis afterward, many commentators claimed that the African American vote was decisive in defeating same-sex marriage in California. According to exit polls, 70 percent of California's African American voters were in favor of Prop 8, compared with 53 percent of Latino voters, 49 percent of Asian voters, and 49 percent of white voters. Op-ed pieces in the LGBT and mainstream press immediately asked why the "black vote"—inaccurately presented as monolithic—was "homophobic."

Even before the voting began, pundits were predicting that black voters would tip the balance in favor of Prop 8 and against same-sex marriage. An analysis in the September 21, 2008, *New*

York Times, "Same-Sex Marriage Ban Is Tied to Obama Factor," argued that then-candidate Barack Obama would be to blame, as the anticipated large African American turnout at the polls would make the passage of Prop 8 more likely.

When Prop 8 did pass, many in the LGBT and mainstream media tried to explain the supposedly higher levels of homophobia among African Americans by pointing to deep, long-standing tensions between the African American and gay communities. This explanation ignored the reality that there are many LGBT people in the African American community and many antiracist, nonblack LGBT people. Popular national advice columnist and news analyst Dan Savage even complained on his blog that, while the LGBT community supported African American civil rights, "I can't help but feeling hurt that the love and support aren't mutual." He went on to write, "I do know this, though: I'm done pretending that the handful of racist gay white men out there—and they're out there, and I think they're scum—are a bigger problem for African Americans, gay and straight, than the huge numbers of homophobic African Americans are for gay Americans, whatever their color."

Other journalists countered this. Hendrik Hertzberg, in the December 1, 2008, *New Yorker*, pointed out that "upward of eighty per cent of Republicans, conservatives, white evangelicals, and weekly churchgoers" voted for Prop 8, and "the initiative would have passed, barely, even if not a single African American had shown up at the polls." Yet, both the liberal and the conservative media refused to let go of the idea that people of color are more homophobic than white people. Liberals were puzzled by what they saw as a contradiction: "Aren't we all fighting for civil rights?" Conservatives seized on a reason to praise the African American community—whom they frequently attack and pathologize as disregarding conventional family formations—for upholding "traditional values."

This discussion rests on a series of untrue presumptions in the popular imagination. The first is that the national LGBT community is mostly white. This is false. It is true, however, that much of the LGBT media, including newspapers, magazines, websites, and blogs, as well as advertising in those places, give the impression that the community is overwhelmingly white. When national and local organizations of color do outreach or promote programs for nonwhite LGBT people, there is often a belief on the part of the white LGBT media that these concerns are, at best, incidental to the presumed, mostly white audience.

The second, very common presumption is that there are a lower percentage of LGBT people in communities of color. In contrast, many LGBT spokespeople have claimed that, while there is no way to actually count who identifies as LGBT in any community, there are probably the same percentage of LGBT-identified people across ethnicities, classes, and races. New polling, however, suggests that there are far more, not fewer, people of color who are openly gay—particularly in comparison with the out, white LGBT population—than studies have previously claimed. A 2012 Gallup poll of 121,290 US citizens showed that, by and large, nonwhite women and men were more likely to identify as LGB than white respondents. For instance, black men between the ages of eighteen and twenty-nine claimed a gay identity at a rate 56 percent higher than white men in the same age group. Hispanic men answered 49 percent higher than their white cohort. And Asian men of similar ages answered 23 percent higher than their white counterparts that they were gay. Polls simply give us a snapshot of their respondents, so it is important not to place too much weight on these results. However, it is clear that there are a sizable number of women and men who identify as LGBT in communities of color.

The third presumption is that marginalized communities, even when their differences are evident, always have exactly shared interests. This ignores the reality of historical and cultural differences, and leads to the sort of sloppy thinking manifested by Dan Savage. When he feels "hurt" because "the love and support aren't mutual," he writes as though there is an agreed-upon system of support and equivalency between groups.

When there are differences of opinion among groups, such as over same-sex marriage, as evidenced in the African American vote in Prop 8, they quickly become an occasion for name-calling and recrimination. It would be far more productive if differences marked a time for beginning realistic, if difficult, discussions between communities.

These differences did not appear overnight. The history of interactions between an evolving LGBT movement and an evolving African American civil rights movement is intricate and complicated. Examining it briefly may clarify how some of the connections and differences between them took shape. In the 1920s, there were prominent African American women and men, many part of the Harlem Renaissance, writing and speaking about homosexuality. Writers such as Wallace Thurman, Angelina Weld Grimke, Alice Dunbar Nelson, Richard Bruce Nugent, and Claude McKay, among others, were known in their literary circles to be homosexual and often wrote about these experiences in both open and coded ways. They were all involved in the larger project of defining new freedoms for African Americans in the United States. The Harlem Renaissance has been described as a civil rights enterprise masquerading as an arts movement.

The openness of the Harlem Renaissance, along with Harlem's very openly gay and lesbian nightlife, was less reflected in the political organizing of that period. Banking on gaining acceptance through respectability, pioneer activists such as W. E. B. Du Bois fostered a strong politic of fitting in that he hoped would "elevate the race." Du Bois fired his longtime friend and co-worker Augustus Granville Dill from the *Crisis*, the NAACP newspaper, after Dill was arrested for having sex in a men's room. (Du Bois later apologized for this in his autobiography.) Interestingly, many thinkers and writers of the Harlem Renaissance distanced themselves from the great, openly bisexual blues singers Bessie Smith and Ma Rainey not because they were too overtly sexual in their work but because blues was considered a vulgar, lower-class art form. Like many other Americans, many in the early African American civil rights movement may have held religious objections to homosexual behavior, but they also pinned their hopes on assimilation and acceptance through imitation of middle-class mores, which prevented a public acceptance of homosexuals. And yet, we know that there were many lesbians and gay men in the civil rights movement. Pacifist and political strategist Bayard Rustin was a confidant of Martin Luther King Jr., and helped organize the 1963 March on Washington. Reverend Pauli Murray was active in the civil rights movement and was the first ordained black woman in the Episcopal Church.

The early gay rights organizations were reformist groups that sought basic protections for homosexuals. While they did not prioritize discussions of race, or what we would now call diversity, many of them had members of color. The Los Angeles–based Knights of the Clock, formed in the late 1940s, focused on the needs of interracial male couples. There were many interracial couples in the Daughters of Bilitis, an early lesbian group formed by Del Martin and Phyllis Lyon, in 1955. In the late 1960s, the radical Gay Liberation Front, very much a product of the social justice movements of its time, focused on issues of racial justice and sought alliances with groups such as the Black Panthers. The Black Panther Party, very concerned with black masculinity, was not always open to these overtures, although its chairman, Huey Newton, did issue what was essentially a personal, remarkable, and strong statement of solidarity with the struggles of homosexual people. But the radicalism of the Gay Liberation Front was short-lived and quickly replaced by a reformist gay rights movement that for many years did not prioritize and often even ignored issues of racial equality and social justice.

Historically, there have been few official alliances between the major, national LGBT groups and coalitions of people of color. Since the 1970s, however, there have been many LGBT people of color who have attempted to analyze and remedy this situation. Lesbian and gay male activists such as Jewelle Gomez, Essex Hemphill, Barbara Smith, Assotto Saint, Audre Lorde, and Gloria Anzaldúa have written passionately and brilliantly on both the racism of the predominantly white LGBT movement and the homophobia present in various communities of color. In her groundbreaking essay "The

Power to Transform: Homophobia in the Black Community," Cheryl Clarke wrote, "Homophobia among black people in America is largely reflective of the homophobic culture in which we live." Her point is not to blame homophobia on mainstream white culture, but to place minority culture in a broader context. She ends the essay by calling for heterosexual African Americans to reach beyond political and religious rhetoric to embrace not only black queer people, but also the goals of the LGBT movement. Clarke argues that not to do so is to "collude with the dominant white male culture to repress not only gay men and lesbians, but also to repress a natural part of all human beings, namely the bisexual potential in us all."[1]

African American LGBT people have discussions about homophobia in their communities, organizations, and churches all the time. To write about the African American community as a monolithic group not only ignores the existence of African American LGBT people. It also seriously misrepresents where and how the fault lines between, and within, communities take shape.

Much of the legislation that has addressed LGBT discrimination over the past forty years has been based on antidiscrimination bills that were designed to protect people of color. Most of these were patterned on the federal Civil Rights Act of 1964. Today, more than twenty states, and close to 150 cities and counties, have enacted laws that ban discrimination in jobs and housing because of a person's perceived or actual sexual orientation. While this is a good example of how discrimination against gay and black people has come to be treated similarly by the law, it does not automatically create connections among the people of these communities.

We all have multiple identities that exist simultaneously. They are based on class background, race, ethnicity, religion, sexual desire, physical and cognitive ability, and even physical appearance. This is not a new idea. Political thinkers, particularly W. E. B. Du Bois, have promulgated it for almost a century. And even he could not accept all the identities it is easier to lay claim to today—such as LGB and, more recently, T. In the late 1960s, black feminists used the idea of an individual's multiple identities to explain their lives and politics. Legal scholar Kimberlé Crenshaw coined the word "intersectionality" in the late 1980s as a metaphor for the ways African American women are affected by multiple, overlapping systems of oppression as both women and people of color.[2] The term subsequently acquired a broader meaning having to do with the multiplicity of everyone's identity.

Intersectionality is not simply a sociological term to explain the complexities of people's lives. It is useful in planning political strategy, as well. Political organizers have learned that political change occurs more quickly and with a firmer and broader base of support if groups with shared self-interests work together. This is called, on a very basic level, coalition building. Intersectionality illustrates the multiple ways and issues around which people can form coalitions.

Nonetheless, if shared self-interest is based on a single identity, such as being gay or black, these identities may become all encompassing and mutually exclusive. Gay people and black people each wonder why the other group doesn't understand their supposed shared conditions of being minorities. But gay and black people may not support each other's causes because other dimensions of their lives, beyond race and sexuality, are, for them, more important to their lived experience. Rather than rely on our traditional understanding of identity politics, it makes more sense to look at how people across groups might connect on a wide range of issues. These might include attention to socioeconomic conditions, health care, or improving access to support programs, such as food assistance, family services, or job training. Working together to attain these goals, which are based on basic human needs, could foster connections between people, or groups of people, that fall outside of the traditional ways of thinking about identity politics.

New forms of social organizing beyond the parameters of identity politics may be needed even more today, at a time of increasing economic uncertainty for so many. For instance, organizing around issues of interpersonal dependency—such as children and the elderly depending upon economically stable adults—would give us a new way to think about how to restructure lives and cultures.[3] Another example, only now being explored by activists or theorists, is how disability status, which every human may eventually claim, might be a useful bond among diverse groups of people, to fight for what all people need for a safe, productive existence.[4] People in very different minority groups may well support the goals of one another not because of shared interest, but because their understanding of the disadvantage and pain of other groups is based on questions of material survival to which everyone can relate. Can you keep a roof over your head? Can you put food on the table? Who will look after you when you are sick or otherwise unable to care for yourself? How will you pay for the doctor and hospital bills?

Even when there are identity-based coalitions that are working, it is important to acknowledge tensions predicated on conflicting political or religious beliefs. For the past few decades, the Congressional Black Caucus (CBC) has been extraordinarily supportive of most of the LGBT antidiscrimination initiatives that have been put forward in Congress, including the repeal of Don't Ask, Don't Tell. The CBC's stance on Don't Ask, Don't Tell was at odds with the views of many African American pastors who had stated their theological opposition to many gay rights issues, especially same-sex marriage. Both the "for" and "against" views were rooted in deeply held beliefs and essentially at odds with each other. There is no problem here; any given community can hold contradictory beliefs. In May 2012, the NAACP, a group very sensitive to a broad range of political and religious sentiments in the African American community, came out in support of marriage equality. It looked past theological questions and framed the issue as a matter of simple equality under the law. Just as important, these examples illustrate that politics is a process that draws on numerous people and points of view.

History, shifting political attitudes, popular sentiments, and economic trends all have made coalitions around LGBT freedom a complicated and continuously evolving process. To focus on whether one minority groups is "more" or "less" homophobic than others is to sidestep the larger, complex issues of lived conditions.

Empathy based simply on identity, or shared social status, such as in the idea that both black people and gay people are oppressed, cannot alone bridge the very different histories of these groups.

Coalitions have to be purposeful and ongoing. Identity politics have been a mainstay of political life and thinking in the United States over the past half century. They have often been effective in bringing about social justice. Sometimes they have gotten in the way of effective change. Maybe it is now time to think of identity politics as a place from which we can begin and then advance, rather than as our final destination.

PART 4

IT'S JUST A PHASE

LESBIANS DO NOT HAVE REAL SEX

Heterosexuals are simultaneously fascinated by and clueless about lesbian sex. "So, what do you do, exactly?" At some point in her life, pretty much any lesbian will be asked this question. Lurking behind this query is a host of assumptions about what constitutes "real sex" and what a "real woman" sexually desires. Sexual agency—the ability to make decisions about what you like to do sexually and then act upon them—has historically been denied to women. Many men (straight and gay) simply cannot imagine that real sex takes place without penetration with a penis. For this reason, lesbian sex has become a cultural marker, a stand-in, for the question "What actually counts as sex?"—for anyone.

There are many ways people, including straight people, have and enjoy sex. Lesbians do not need a penis to have penetrative sex. Some lesbians use dildos for penetration; other do not, preferring fingers, hands, fists, tongues. However, culturally, we refer to a very particular sexual act—penis in vagina—as, simply, sex. Consider the expression "losing your virginity." This commonly means the first experience of heterosexual genital intercourse. This definition is so instilled in our culture as "sex" that many heterosexual teenagers do not consider oral sex and anal sex "real sex." Even if they engage in these forms of sexual activity, they still understand themselves to be virgins. (This may be particularly true for women, who have been told that their virginity confirms their virtue.) Recall then-president Bill Clinton's infamous assertion, during the scandal over Monica Lewinsky, that he "did not have sex with that woman." Clinton's hairsplitting legalism was made possible because the sex in question was oral sex. In this hierarchy of sexual acts, heterosexual genital intercourse sits at the top. Other body parts (such as the mouth and anus) and other sexual acts (such as oral sex, anal sex, manual sex, and masturbation) may be extremely pleasurable, but are seen only as warm-ups to the real thing. This very limited definition of sex prevents people from recognizing lesbian sex as real sex. At best, what lesbians do is foreplay that can never reach completion on its own. Or, it is a turn-on for straight men and a staple of heterosexual pornography. A scene of two women kissing—increasingly common on mainstream television in shows such as *Gossip Girl* and *Community*—is often used to add titillation to an otherwise mundane plot. As long as the women involved are conventionally pretty and feminine, this lesbianism is safe and sexy for prime-time viewing. (Butch women, by contrast, are often seen as erotic turn-offs: unsexy imitations of real men.) In each of these scenarios, lesbian sex is something women do while they are waiting for a man to come along. The straight male viewer, the target audience for "lesbian" pornography, is invited to imagine himself into the scene, as the one who can complete the picture and turn the warm-up act into the real deal.

The problem here is not pornography or television. It is how one particular set of sexual fantasies is set up as a universal fantasy and reality. Sexual fantasies can be powerful and important, and pornography—like many other forms of representation—is a vehicle for sexual fantasizing. However, there is a potential problem when fantasy bodies and acts are accepted by large numbers of people to be the truth about what a lesbian is and what all women really want. This worldview is extremely narrow and limited. It does not acknowledge the diversity of ways women have sex with one another or the variety of female bodies.

Confusing pornography—or any depictions of sex in entertainment—with reality can lead straight as well as LGBT people to have unrealistic expectations of what sex looks like and feels like. As queer sex educator Tristan Taormino states, Hollywood, Madison Avenue, and the porn industry have all sold us ridiculously unrealistic images of flawless bodies and red-hot sex.[1] Everyday life is much more complicated, but has a difficult time competing with a fantasy.

The distorting effects of these fantasies do not shape all of us with equivalent force. Lesbians must contend with a male-centered view of what they would or should want if they met the right man. Bisexual and straight women also suffer when their sexuality is continuously placed in scenarios in which it exists only for heterosexual men's pleasure. But the most dangerous implication of this myth is that the right man could show a lesbian what she really wants and turn her straight.

Many lesbians have had sex with men, either before they came out or while they were coming out. Sex with a man did not change or prevent their lesbianism. Some self-identified lesbians still have occasional sex with men, and this does not make them heterosexual or bisexual.

Nevertheless, the myth that sex with the right man could make a lesbian go straight persists and can take deadly form, such as "corrective" or "punitive rape." Corrective rape is a violent sexual assault in which a person is targeted because of her sexual or gender nonconformity. The term came into use after the brutal gang rape and murder of openly lesbian South African soccer star Eudy Simelane, in 2008. South African LGBT activists began to track incidence of these crimes against lesbians and to organize against this violence both domestically and internationally. The problem is hardly confined to South Africa. Cases have been documented in Thailand, Zimbabwe, Canada, and the United States.[2]

"Corrective" here suggests that the reason for a particular assault is the perpetrator's desire to fix the victim's "incorrect" identity. This is misleading. There is nothing to correct. Additionally, the violent assault is motivated as much, if not more, by the perpetrator's rage at the target's perceived sexual or gender deviance. It is a punishment for the victim's transgressing accepted gender or sexual norms. The term "punitive rape" thus more accurately describes the larger social context of such assaults. In 2011, the United Nations High Commissioner for Human Rights declared that they are "[p]art of a wider pattern of sexual violence" that "combine[s] a fundamental lack of respect for women, often amounting to misogyny, with deeply-entrenched homophobia."[3]

Although their actions are extreme, the perpetrators of punitive rape are expressing views—about the naturalness of heterosexuality, for example, and men's authority over women—held by many people. Most people who hold these beliefs do not rape lesbians. Nevertheless, this violence exists on a continuum with the everyday and, to many people, innocuous prejudices evident in such myths as lesbians do not have real sex.

This "innocuous" violence is embedded in the idea of virginity. Historically, the very idea of "virginity" emerged from the religious and social regulations of a marriage contract. Through marriage, a woman was exchanged as property from her father to her husband. Her chastity guaranteed that her property value was intact. The deeply entrenched belief that it takes a man for a woman to lose her virginity begins here. Women have long tried to assert their own sexual desires, but their voices are still not completely acknowledged in many places globally, including the United States.

One of this myth's ironies is that lesbians themselves have engaged in sometimes-pitched battles over a related question: what counts as real lesbian sex? This is not a disagreement over whether or not lesbians have real sex. These arguments are over the centrality of sex to lesbian identity and what constitutes the proper, correct kind of lesbian sex within lesbian feminist political communities.

These questions arose decades ago and are rooted in fights within the just-forming women's movement of the early 1970s. Lesbians were very active in what has come to be known as "second-wave" feminism and fought for recognition of lesbian equality as a feature of sexual equality. But many straight feminists, such as National Organization for Women founder Betty Friedan, were leery of a close association with lesbianism. They worried that the "lavender menace" would discredit feminism.

In the midst of these battles, poet Adrienne Rich published her 1980 essay "Compulsory Heterosexuality and Lesbian Existence."[4] Rich was responding powerfully to heterosexual feminists who ignored lesbians or who marginalized the lesbian experience. Rejecting mainstream culture's obsession with girl-on-girl action, Rich de-emphasized genital sexuality and argued that intense same-sex bonds between women were the heart of lesbianism. Coining the term "lesbian continuum," she described the multiple forms of nonheterosexual, independent, women-focused resistance that women have always undertaken to combat patriarchy. While this resistance included explicitly sexual ties between women, Rich believed that sex between women was not in and of itself feminist political resistance. Her elaboration of a lesbian continuum was a brilliant conceptual coup that converted lesbianism from a marginal position to a global narrative of women's resistance.

Some feminists misconstrued the subtlety and context of Rich's arguments. This led to a glorification of the desexualized lesbian. Woman-woman bonds were celebrated, while woman-woman sex was downplayed.

The sisterly ties imagined by Rich frayed very quickly. Disagreements among feminists over the politics of sexuality came to a head during the so-called feminist "sex wars" of the 1980s.[5] Over the course of this decade, feminists—lesbian, bisexual, and straight—disagreed vehemently over sexual issues such as pornography, heterosexuality, butch/femme gender roles, and sadomasochism. After a decade of avoiding difficult sexual discussions, feminists found themselves embroiled in bitter debates over the borders between pleasure and danger and between politically correct and politically incorrect sex.[6] Sex had become the defining issue for feminist politics.

During the sex wars, some aspects of lesbian sexual culture—mainly butch/femme gender roles and sadomasochism—were criticized for allegedly imitating heterosexuality. Many lesbians—such as Esther Newton, Joan Nestle, Amber Hollibaugh, and Cherrie Moraga—argued against this.[7] They saw butch/femme as a distinctively lesbian way of transgressing and undermining gender and sexual norms.

Other lesbians made similar arguments for the transgressive potential of S/M to play with and rework power inequalities. In 1978, Gayle Rubin and Pat (now Patrick) Califia even founded the first lesbian-feminist organization dedicated to sadomasochism, Samois, which became instantly controversial, its members accused of eroticizing violence against women.[8]

At the end of the 1980s, another battle in the lesbian sex wars erupted, this time over dildo use. The arguments took a by-now familiar form. Some lesbians claimed that dildos and strap-ons were authentically lesbian; others decried their use as male-identified.

The sex wars, for all their rancor, provided a very valuable, public airing of the enormous diversity that exists among lesbians when it comes to sexual identity, sexual pleasure, and, especially, gender identification. Some lesbians prefer a butch/femme dyad, others do not. Today, there is a far wider acknowledged spectrum of lesbian gender than traditional butch/femme roles. This is especially true for younger women coming out and exploring new identities: androgynous, boi, tomboy, girl-next-door, butch at the edge of trans, dandy, soccer mom. It is not simply that you cannot always tell a lesbian just by looking, but rather what a lesbian looks like does not tell you anything about the sexual roles or activities she prefers. Not every butch is a sexual top. Not every femme is a sexual bottom. There is no one way to be a lesbian and have sex with other women.

Despite all this variety in lesbian experience and self-presentation, lesbians still remain caught between two opposing mainstream stereotypes: the hypersexual (and hyperfeminine) lesbians of heterosexual entertainments and the asexual lesbians who bring a U-Haul to their second date. These opposing stereotypes of lesbian sexuality reflect the opposing sexual stereotypes placed on all women. They are either whores or virgins. But the implications of these stereotyping efforts go beyond female sexuality and lesbianism. If lesbians represent the most extreme form of female sexual passivity, gay men represent male sexuality at its most out of control and are even pathologized as sex addicts.

At least gay men—as men—are still imagined to be interested, albeit overly so, in sex. The myth of sexless lesbian couples—colorfully captured in the phrase "lesbian bed death"—is as demeaning as the media-fueled image of lesbians gone wild. In both instances, women's sexuality is seen as something to be activated for straight men or it is no activity at all. Lesbians themselves joke about U-Hauls and lesbian bed death, but as an inside joke, not science.

The term "lesbian bed death" was coined by sociologists Philip Blumstein and Pepper Schwartz in their 1983 book *American Couples: Money, Work, Sex*. Blumstein and Schwartz wrote that long-term lesbian couples have significantly less sex and intimacy than both gay male and heterosexual couples. Their data have since been widely challenged. In fact, all long-term couples seem to experience a decline in sexual frequency. Lesbian couples show no more marked a decline than others. Still, the end result of this idea is that a widespread sexual phenomenon has been denied—erased—by naming it as a uniquely lesbian experience. The myth of lesbian bed death refuses to die because it is simply a new version of the penis-centered logic propelling the myth that lesbian sex is not real sex.

This myth is also powerfully fueled by the sad reality that our culture is pretty terrible at talking about sex and sexual pleasure. There is little public or private acknowledgment that what we want to do sexually often changes across our lifetime and everyday circumstances. This should not be surprising. Bodies change over time, as do emotional and psychological needs, sometimes regularly. A preference for penetration becomes a preference for oral sex, or vice versa. A desire to be exclusively a top or a bottom becomes a desire to take turns. A preference for younger women may become an attraction to older women. Some women like to sleep together before dating or sleep together without ever dating. Different sexual cultures and identities—which may change generationally or be markedly different in urban, suburban, or rural settings—also give new meaning to sex acts.

A simple reality—the fact that when it comes to sex, people are different from each other,⁹ and can even differ from their own earlier selves—is obscured by people's need to overgeneralize their own desires and discomforts. To paraphrase Gayle Rubin, one person's most treasured erotic activity might be another person's major turnoff.¹⁰ In our culture, almost all people lack a language to capture the full reality of their sex lives and fantasies. It just happens the way we want it, or it doesn't. We're satisfied, and then we're not. This may be a version of turning lemons into lemonade, but sexual minorities—people whose sexual desires, identities, and practices differ from the norm—do a better job talking about sex, precisely because they are constantly asked to explain and justify their love and their lust to a wider culture and, even, to themselves. Lesbians know how to bring on the lemonade, with many twists. Whether in a long-term relationship, casual hookup, or one-night stand, lesbian sex can be as hot and throbbing or as boring and predictable as anyone else's. Which is to say, very real.

MYTH 14

ALL BISEXUAL MEN ARE ACTUALLY GAY; ALL BISEXUAL WOMEN ARE ACTUALLY STRAIGHT

Most people eagerly, and happily, embrace a sexual identity. Whether gay, lesbian, or straight, these identities, to a large degree, clear up a lot of confusion and often bring understanding, acceptance, and comfort to the people who claim them and to those around them. Everybody knows where they are on the map of who wants whom. But one sexual identity seems to lead to confusion: bisexual. This term is often—but not always—claimed by men and women who desire both men and women.

In the popular imagination, people are presumed to desire either men or women. This method of sorting people's desires controls and manages sexuality by eliminating gray areas. In reality, sexuality overflows such specific categories. It often refuses to be contained by social conventions and cultural certainties. Many people who identify as bisexual may desire one sex more than another. Others would say they desire men and women about equally. A bisexual person might desire both men and women, or desire men for a period of time and then women. Bisexuality offers a language for describing the fluidity of desire.

However, this ambiguity generates anxiety and condescension, often directed at bisexual people. We suppose, and often insist, that we know exactly what we do and do not want sexually. No wonder that bisexuals pose a problem. The two statements in this myth regarding bisexuality—that bisexual men are actually gay, and bisexual women are actually straight—are really saying the same thing: bisexuals can't seem to make up their minds about whether they like men or women.

Popular understandings and representations of bisexuality operate firmly within a system of two distinct genders. Because this gender binary quickly becomes a gender hierarchy, there are very different social rules and cultural expectations for bisexual men and bisexual women. When a woman is sexually available to at least one man, no matter how many women she has sex with, she gets placed back into the category of heterosexuality. Her sexual relationships with other women are not taken seriously (see myth 13, "Lesbians Do Not Have Real Sex"). Women are typically seen as sexual objects rather than as subjects capable of exercising agency and autonomy in their sexual choices. This leads to the cultural delusion that any woman who is attractive to a man must be, at some level, straight because she has incited his desire.

On the other hand, men who are attracted to men suffer a status loss by challenging the sexual supremacy of all men who desire women. In a culture that identifies male homosexuality with the feminine, sex with another man could contaminate all masculinity unless it is quarantined in some way. For bisexual men, the assumption is one gay strike and you're out. This serves to preserve the fiction of a secure and stable male heterosexuality (see myth 5, "Most Homophobes Are Repressed Homosexuals").

Self-identified bisexuals have been trapped in this two-sided myth since "bisexual" was first widely claimed as an identity during the sexual liberation movements of the late 1960s and 1970s. Since that time, the idea of bisexuality has had a complicated journey through American culture. A 1974 article in *Time* magazine, "The New Bisexuals," listed factors other than women's desire itself as causes of female bisexuality. These included the revelations of the Kinsey studies, feminism, and "the emphasis by [sex therapists] Masters and Johnson, among others, on the clitoral orgasm that has led to more sexual experimentation." In the 1970s, the concept of bisexuality was touted by the media as an edgy new lifestyle personified by glam rock superstars, nightclubbing at trendy discos, and a let-it-all-hang-out ethos.[1] Numerous celebrities were associated with bisexuality, with some openly claiming the identity, such as Janis Joplin. Other celebrities became associated with bisexuality because they represented a kind of omnivorous sexuality: everybody wanted them. Whether their devoted fans wanted to be them or have them sexually was an open question. Performers such as Mick Jagger, David Bowie, and Grace Jones presented themselves as open to any sexual stimulus. Suspecting or even knowing a particular celebrity was bisexual was not the same thing as knowing whom and how she or he actually loved, desired, and organized a life. These celebrities were mirrors of their fans' desires and fantasies, not the truth of bisexuality.

The era of 1970s bisexual chic may have faded, but it's still with us today in less flamboyant ways. In recent years, many Hollywood celebrities and pop stars, such as Madonna, Sandra Bernhard, Angelina Jolie, Drew Barrymore, Alan Cumming, Anna Paquin, and Lady Gaga, have either come out as bisexual or been labeled as such by the media. Many men's magazines, such as *Complex* and *COED*, feature lists and photos of the hottest female bisexual celebrities, meant to inspire fantasies of lesbian sex for the magazines' readers. And think of the titillating covers of the *National Enquirer* "exposing" the bisexual history of stars such as Lindsay Lohan and Tila Tequila. Tequila built an entire reality show around the drama of her bisexuality: would she choose a woman or a man from the suitors vying for her hand? Celebrity culture simultaneously popularizes bisexual identity and perpetuates clouds of confusion as to its meaning.

Bisexuality can mean so many different things to so many different people that it can lead to the idea that it is a sexuality out of control. This is a common stereotype all bisexuals confront. If they desire both men and women, they could never be monogamous with anyone. This thinking imagines bisexuals as sexually immature, unable or unwilling to commit to any one person because they cannot commit to one, stable sexual desire.

There are echoes of this accusation of immaturity in the claim that bisexuality is just a phase. The presumption is that eventually all bisexuals will grow into a more mature sexuality, gay or straight. This same infantilization of bisexual people also helps shape the popular perception, and fear, that their desires are dangerously selfish. As the AIDS epidemic grew in the United States during the 1980s, both gay and straight people distanced themselves from bisexual men, accusing them of spreading HIV from gay men to straight women. This is still true today in uninformed and fear-driven public discussions about men on the "down low" who have sex with men but don't identify as gay. These panicked and judgmental discussions about the down low are frequently featured on television talk shows and in many women's magazines. The message here is clearly that men who can't decide on their sexual desires are not to be trusted.

In lived experience, bisexuality comprises the complexity of any person's sexuality, independent of the outside perceptions of others. When it comes to the actual life of desire—what people do, versus what they say—there is certainly a lot more bisexual experience of some kind than is reflected in the number of people who identify as bisexual. Many straight people have a history of bisexual activity but do not identify as "bi." Sexologist Alfred Kinsey demonstrated this in the 1940s and 1950s. His studies indicate that the huge, exclusively heterosexual majority was a lie. Almost half of all people in the United States were aroused by both sexes or had engaged in both homosexual and heterosexual behavior at some point in their lives (see myth 2, "About 10 Percent of People Are Gay or Lesbian").

Our memories confirm this. Many straight men and women

first learn to love, open up, and let go in the context of passionate same-sex friendships, and even erotic same-sex crushes. These early same-sex passions may or may not have involved sex, but they can and do help us learn what we find pleasurable and why we are attracted to people. Sometimes desire can be stirred by seeing and wanting people who are like us in gender or sexual expression. Sometimes we desire people who are very different from us. People can also be attractive to others for how their gender combines masculinity and femininity. There are masculine men who are attracted to more-masculine-looking women and others who are attracted to more-feminine-looking men. Is this being attracted to a mix of male and female qualities in one person a form of bisexuality? One early and influential understanding of bisexuality—advanced by Sigmund Freud—focused on the co-presence of male and female characteristics in one person. Everyone, Freud argued, was in this sense bisexual. Whom they desired—men or women—reflected the particular balance of this mix in them and the other person.

All too often, though, early same-sex relationships do not fit with later experiences and self-identifications. The formative role they play in the later loves of straight people gets written out. Consider the different kind of pressure experienced by many gay people, who may feel constrained never to mention their childhood cross-sex crushes lest that somehow make people think they are not really gay—a risk for gay men and lesbians in a culture that prefers everybody be straight. Does this mean that the straight person with a same-sex crush or friendship in his or her past is really bisexual? Or that the gay person with a history of cross-sex crushes is as well? You would have to ask those people. Identities mean different things to different people, and they do not explain any person's entire sexuality. For example, a woman who identifies as lesbian may have slept with men in her past. She might even do so occasionally in her present. Does this history trump how she self-identifies? If so, who decides?

People may edit out such passionate bisexual lessons in how to love from their histories of desire for much the same reason others may claim their bisexuality. This is due to changing social and cultural circumstances. One half of a heterosexual couple might be same-sex-attracted or curious to erotically explore with someone of the same sex. The opposite might be true within same-sex couples. People in these situations may explain their feelings, to themselves and others, by saying they are bisexual. But they might not say that to everyone for fear of embarrassment or of being judged. Alternatively, identifying as bisexual is sometimes a transitional stage to claiming a heterosexual or homosexual identity. Many gay men identify as bisexual for fear of being stigmatized as gay and as a way to ease their transition into a gay identity. They are not simply confused about what they really want and really are. Many bisexuals might even identify as gay for political reasons when in the company of straight people, but might identify as bi when talking to biphobic gay people.

Bisexual men and women continue to organize on college campuses, form support groups, and argue—sometimes in the face of openly hostile lesbians and gay men—that they are not undecided, but people with a clearly defined identity. This does not settle the question of what bisexuality is. How bisexuals think, feel, desire, and act is different for every bisexual—just as it is for everyone else. Bisexuality is no messier than other forms of sexual identity or desire.

Bisexual identity brings into the open features common to all sexual desire and identities. That erotic life is far more varied and variable than the tidy identity boxes we check off does not mean that everyone is really bisexual. The ongoing social resonance and currency of bisexuality in our culture, whether we are resistant to it or comfortable with it, demonstrate that none of us, no matter how we self-identify, wants to lose out on where our desires might lead us. Perhaps allowing for the multiple realities of bisexual identity and experience can teach us something about the rich surprises sexual desire can offer over the course of a lifetime.

MYTH 15

TRANSGENDER PEOPLE ARE GAY

The belief that transgender people are gay emerges, paradoxically, from the often-unarticulated belief that gay people are, in some way, transgender. For example, women who desire women (when they should be desiring men) are somehow reversing the natural order of desire. Therefore, they must be reversing the natural order of gender, as well; they must be mannish and not real women. Here, heterosexuality is the final proof of true gender identity. The prominence of the myth that transgender people are gay clearly reflects a presumption that a person's gender is firmly connected to what she or he likes to do in bed—and with whom.

But the existence and experience of transgender people complicate these equations. Transgender people challenge what it means to be a man or woman, gay or straight, masculine or feminine. They also disrupt the seamless series of connections made in our culture between biological sex, gender identity, how we present gender through gender roles, and whom we sexually desire.

These are not new questions; people were discussing them almost one hundred fifty years ago. In the mid-nineteenth century, the Austro-Hungarian lawyer Karl Heinrich Ulrichs claimed that male homosexuality was the result of a "feminine soul enclosed in a male body." This description, with the genders reversed, was also used to explain female homosexuality. In the early twentieth century, influential British psychologist Havelock Ellis continued this tradition of associating inside-out, or inverted, gender with homosexual desire, and coined the term "sexual inversion" as the likely cause of homosexuality. Believing that homosexuals were born with the soul of the "opposite sex," these sexologists argued that some inner essence, rather than your external biological sex, determined whom you might sexually desire.

This reasoning may seem simplistic, or even metaphysical, to us today. Yet the idea that sexual desire exists in relation to a soul, and not just a body, accurately describes the experiences of many transgender people, as well as gay men and lesbians today. Many lesbians and gay men report that their own childhood gender nonconformity (as a tomboy or sissy boy) was often the first clue for the later discovery of their homosexuality. But when they're older, tomboys can become lipstick lesbians and sissy boys can become hypermasculine gay men.

Sexual desire and gender expression intersect in different ways for different people. Rules regulating gender behavior are based in culture and change over time (see myth 3, "All Transgender People Have Sex-Reassignment Surgery"). They are also about more than what we do on the outside. As rules about gender change, they open up new ways for us to live in our bodies, understand ourselves, and interact with others.

Bodies are very important to people. They are a huge part of how we live in the world and think about gender and sexuality. People commonly think that the biological differences of the sexes are a simple matter of distinguishing penis from vagina, sperm from egg, men from women. But biology is far more complex—and less simply divided—than many people believe. Bodies are complicated, and biological differences between bodies are interpreted by scientists who live in a world in which bodies and identities get divided into two: male and female. These cultural frameworks shape what scientists can see and how they interpret their knowledge.

People conflate sexual desire with gender identity because gender presentation is often linked to biological traits, such as body curves, body hair, and vocal range. Many people, gay and straight, are attracted to these particular sexual traits, which usually appear very differently in men and women and are identified with masculinity or femininity. When any person, scientist or not, makes decisive arguments about biological sex, often what they are really talking about is gender.[1] Not only can the meaning of sexual traits change, but people can change the sexual traits of their bodies. In this way, transgender people force dominant culture to rethink a lot of its basic assumptions about the lineup among biological sex, gender identity, and sexuality. Neither the bodies we have nor the bodies we aspire to attain through sex-reassignment surgery or other modifications reliably predict the bodies we sexually desire.

The Lives of Transgender People, a comprehensive social survey by Genny Beemyn and Susan Rankin, focuses on many aspects of transgender people's lives, including how sexual orientation relates to gender transition. They write, "Slightly more than one third of the FTM/T [female-to-male/transgender] participants characterized their sexual orientation as 'other,' 28 percent identified as heterosexual, and 20 percent identified as bisexual. . . . The majority of these 'other' respondents described themselves as queer or pansexual."[2] Every participant's story is unique, but the findings here suggest something fascinating. Those who indicated their sexual orientation as queer or pansexual may not have been comfortable with the sexual identity categories heterosexual or homosexual that typically mark male or female gender. Transgender people challenge the clear definitions of gender that are the basis for the identities homosexual and heterosexual. At least for female-to-male transpeople, changing genders opened up new possibilities for understanding, naming, and enacting their sexual desires as well.

The findings for transgender people who were born male show something different: "Among MTF/transgender . . . , the predominant sexual orientations were bisexual (respectively 36 percent and 38 percent) and heterosexual (respectively 29 percent and 24 percent)."[3] These findings suggest that the sexual attractions of male-to-female transpeople more often remain defined around traditional sexual identity categories than is the case for female-to-male transpeople.

These differences may connect to the fact that women in our culture are often granted more social permission to depart from standard ideals of femininity than men are from masculinity. Some social scientists, with considerable evidence, also believe that women are more sexually fluid than men. Do these factors influence transpeople as they form new sexual and gender identities during and after transitioning? We must be cautious not to hypothesize too much from a single study. Some MTFs who were married to women prior to their transition may continue to identify as heterosexual post-transition. They may even remain married to their wives.[4] This is not about maintaining masculine privileges, because a change in gender identity does not mandate a change in sexual identity or in life partner. The paths followed by each transperson will be different, and may also be forged in relation to loved others.

The reality is that transgender people can both uphold and dismantle gender norms at the same time. They raise profound questions about the amount of autonomy people have to define their gender and sexual identities and remake their bodies. These are important questions that all humans face across their lives. Changing your gender or presenting it in nontraditional ways may be socially liberating for yourself and for some people with whom you interact. It may also be very threatening.

Paradoxically, the myth that transgender people are really gay may be a nervous reaction to the many ways in which gay and transgender people are not the same. It is a way for both gay and straight people to ward off all the complicated permutations of difference in the world. The myth may also block grappling with the very real implications these differences have for how we live together in both productive and destructive ways.

The oversimplification of differences between LGB and T people has led to political stalemates and often to the misunderstanding and vilification of transgender people. Over the years, many gay men and lesbians have sought to distance themselves from transgender people. This has fueled mainstream political culture's attack on those who are transgender. With increasing frequency, we have seen traditional antigay rhetoric being used to describe transgender people. In the main, political campaign ads against gay people have become less vitriolic and more subtle since the 1970s. The opposite is true where transpeople and transgender rights are concerned. In recent years, political ads have appeared arguing that it is transgender people, rather than gay people, who are child molesters. These ads depict transpeople, especially MTFs, as grotesque, hairy-bodied musclemen cross-dressing in the company of children.[5]

Violence against gay people has often been aimed at those who are nonnormative in their gender presentation. Butch lesbians, drag queens, mannish women, and effeminate men have always borne the brunt of antigay violence. Whatever your sexual desire, it is visible gender deviance that prompts punishing violence. According to the National Coalition of Anti-Violence Programs, in 2011, anti-transgender bias accounted for 14 percent of all reported hate violence incidents. Of the thirty murders classified as hate violence, 40 percent were of transgender women. Transgender people were 1.74 times as likely to experience discrimination as nontransgender people and 1.58 times as likely to experience injuries because of hate violence. The numbers rise sharply for transgender people of color, who were 28 percent more likely to experience physical violence. These rates are extraordinarily high, considering that recent studies have estimated that transgender-identified people are only 0.3 percent of the US population. The actual number of transpeople targeted for violence is probably far higher. Hate violence against transgender people is the most underreported segment of violence against LGBT people, because of stigma and a lack of resources. As Beemyn and Rankin conclude in their study, transgender people who identify as straight are less likely to report harassment. This may be because straight-identified transpeople are more likely to try to pass as the "opposite sex" and thus not appear gender deviant.

These very real concerns make it crucial to think carefully about how and why people continually connect gender nonconformity and homosexuality. The feminist and sexual liberation movements have challenged social and religious beliefs about sex and desire and changed the world in which we live. Gender theory has allowed us to understand it in new ways. Together they open up new political and social possibilities for how all people can live in their bodies in ways that feel right and true to them. They also complicate strongly held beliefs about the biological nature of sexuality and sex differences.

As important as these changes and ideas are, they cannot eradicate our binary way of thinking about sex and its consequences at all levels. Both sexual desire and gender are shaped in relation to the very real differences in the reproductive capacities of male and female bodies. These biological differences need not determine either gender or sexual identity. Humans have always exhibited wildly different and richly textured approaches to their experiences of bodily capacities, gender, and sexual desire. This ability has allowed them to grow, and to survive in the world.

The relationship between gay and transgender people is one of social and political survival. Gay and transgender people have sought one another's support because they could not find it in environments, such as schools and workplaces, that are hostile to those who deviate from heterosexual gender norms. These alliances thrive in alternative social circumstances—gay-straight alliances, bars and clubs, political groups such as the National Gay and Lesbian Task Force, or individual friendships—that allow and celebrate difference. It is because difference exists between people that we can, and must, find affinities across sexuality and gender to generate life-sustaining, and flourishing, possibilities for their expression.

THERE'S NO SUCH THING
AS A GAY OR TRANS CHILD

Over the past two decades, more and more young people have been declaring, and at younger and younger ages, that they are gay or trans. But these gay and trans youth are consistently told that their feelings are not real and will just go away. Some parents fear that if mainstream culture accepts same-sex desire and gender non-conformity as normal, healthy, and positive, their children may be encouraged to engage in it. They are correct. Different models of sexual behavior and gender, especially the widespread visibility of LGBT identities, do offer new ways for people of all ages to behave and identify themselves. The increase in children actively identifying as trans is a direct result of the greater cultural visibility of transgender adults since the mid-1990s.[1]

This is more than a question of identity, and adults know it. Think about all the work parents and educators put into teaching children how to be proper young men and women and shielding them from sexually explicit material. This considerable labor reveals the fear that underlies the myth that there are no gay or trans children: a child, especially your own, might somehow become gay or trans. Given this cultural tension, it is not surprising that when young people assert that they are gay or trans, many adults become very nervous and upset. Clearly, these young people not only know too much about sex and gender, but they know far too much about the wrong forms of sex and gender—and are willing to say so publicly.

The best way to silence the voices of children and ensure they grow up the "right way" is to create a special social category around them that adults control. This may sound odd to us now, but it is exactly what has happened. In the not-so-distant past, adults created this category. It is called childhood. Conceiving of childhood as a separate phase of life is a distinctly modern way of defining an individual by age. In his 1962 landmark book *Centuries of Childhood*, Philippe Ariès dates the invention of the child to the eighteenth and nineteenth centuries.

To suggest that childhood is an invention does not mean that young people did not previously exist. During earlier historical periods, Western society thought differently about what young people were capable of doing, how they were held responsible, with whom they could socialize, and what games were age appropriate. Before modern childhood was invented, young people were treated more as miniature adults who were considered capable of making adult decisions (and held responsible for doing so) and were not shielded from the realities of sexual activity and reproduction. Over the course of the seventeenth and eighteenth centuries, the idea of "childhood innocence"—that is, children being innocent of adult experience and sexual knowledge—came into being and solidified as a fact in the nineteenth century.

By the twentieth century, psychologist G. Stanley Hall had invented the concept of adolescence, understood as a later phase of childhood even though adolescents looked and acted more like adults. Adolescence effectively extended the time given young people to develop the self-control necessary to meet the coming demands of adulthood. (If they still didn't conform, they could be put into yet another category: juvenile delinquent, which frequently included adolescents who were homosexual or gender deviant.) Ironically, this process often infantilized children and adolescents, making them less mature and less autonomous. They frequently became worrisome and needed to be controlled, apparently for their own good. This battle to regulate children and adolescents continues today, particularly in regard to gender and sexuality (see myth 8, "LGBT Parents Are Bad for Children").

In past years, prior to the emergence of young people identifying as trans, most children who manifested some form of gender nonconformity were presumed to be at risk of growing up gay. This was especially so for boys, whose range of proper gender behavior was more constricting than girls'. Tomboys are often culturally valorized; the sissy is never a hero. Beginning in 1980, both could be diagnosed with gender identity disorder in childhood (see myth 6, "Transgender People Are Mentally Ill").

Childhood gender nonconformity can have little to do with how a person later identifies sexually. Some lesbian and gay men report that their childhood gender deviance was an indicator of their adult sexual desires, but others report the opposite. The larger problem here is the widespread denial in our culture that children, before they identify as gay, straight, bisexual or trans, have sexual feelings, and that these feelings are an active part of their lives and their growing up.

Many adults consider puberty the beginning of an individual's sexuality. Puberty is the name for the broad and varying period of time, roughly between the ages of ten and seventeen for girls and twelve and eighteen for boys, when bodies change and secondary sex characteristics—such as body hair and breasts—emerge. At this age, most boys and girls become capable of sexual reproduction. The popular imagination equates reproductive ability with sexuality—so children being sexual before puberty can't even be a question. Then why, as a culture, are we simultaneously suggesting otherwise? We scold sexually curious children and create cultural panics about sexting and adolescents having sex at younger and younger ages. Despite what many parents and other adults would like to believe, sexuality exists from birth to puberty, and its presence enormously shapes our sexual identities as adults.

What does sexuality look like in children before puberty? One of the first, and most groundbreaking, assertions that children are sexual beings was made by Sigmund Freud. In his 1905 *Three Essays on the Theory of Sexuality*, Freud claimed that, contrary to popular ideals of the innocent, unknowing child, children were deeply curious about sex, explored their bodies, played with their genitals, had sexual fantasies, and could experience sexual pleasure.

Children make sense of these evolving desires and experiences of bodily pleasure in a variety of ways. They often know them only to be pleasurable, and see nothing wrong with them. Adults often have a more conflicted mix of feelings about sexuality, gender, and their bodies. They may experience pleasure and joy from sex, but they may also feel guilt, anxiety, and shame. They may feel a mixture of all of these at any given time. Unfortunately, these adult confusions and ambivalences are often communicated to children. If adults see a child touching herself, do they communicate to her that it is wrong, shameful, or sinful? Or do they communicate some version of, "Honey, it's wonderful to explore your body, but it's also a private thing, so be sure to do that when you are alone"? These two parental responses may create vastly different experiences of sexual desire and psychological self-confidence in children.

Parental authority over children is one of the most important reasons why society denies that children can be gay or trans. Many parents want to raise their children to emulate their own values, social ideas, and ways of viewing the world. With gay and trans issues in social media, television, advertising, and even political coverage, parents may feel the need to exert even more control over their children. We can see this in campaigns to protect children from homosexuality, usually promoted by conservative religious groups such as Focus on the Family. Many parents insist that heterosexuality is the only acceptable route to happiness. They never seriously consider the needs, and desires, of the child. This only protects, and secures, the existing social order for the comfort of adults.

Parental control of gay and trans children happens on a large-scale, organized level. In the early 2000s, the conservative Christian ex-gay movement began targeting younger and younger teenagers to stifle their supposedly unwanted same-sex desires. They are now creating ministries and reparative-therapy groups to help transgender people transition "back." In 2005, fifteen-year-old Zach Stark became a cause célèbre after his parents, upon learning he was gay, forced him to attend an ex-gay camp, Love in Action (now called Restoration Path), against his will. His parents told him he was gay because they had "messed up." Ex-gay camp was supposed to help clear things up. Stark blogged on his MySpace page about his experiences, and his story went viral, garnering great sympathy for him and exposing the enormous injustice of the situation. Stark started at the camp—and even enjoyed some of the other young women and men there—but eventually left and happily claimed his gay male identity.

This gross abuse of parental authority is not restricted to conservative Christians. Many nonreligious parents send their children to therapy to help them "get over" their same-sex attractions. (Some parents, to their credit, offer their children support, even using gay-friendly therapists to make sure that they have additional emotional help in the face of potential bullying.)

Parents' panic over a gay or trans child is really a panic that they produced the wrong kind of child. Parents might also be ashamed at what their neighbors and friends would say or think if they knew their child was gay or trans. Acknowledging a gay or trans child may be difficult for parents, especially if they live in a socially or religiously conservative community. But there is no doubt that all of this is much more difficult on the child. Denying children their sexual or gender identities, indeed their human right to be gay or trans, is not guidance, oversight, education, or instruction. It is abuse. All children have a difficult time growing up. They have little power, little agency, little freedom, no ability to be independent, and are almost entirely at the mercy of their parents. Beyond the intense expectations and anxieties of the adults around them, children are also routinely subject to their own fears, hopes, and fantasies. But no one asks straight children "when they knew" they were straight.

The question here is not if children understand their sexuality or gender at a young age. It is how they understand it. How we name people, experiences, feelings, actions, and mental states matters a lot. This has been true of the classification "childhood." It has been true of the terms "gay" and "trans." It matters because it shapes people's lives in many concrete ways. It matters because it helps organize how people think about a topic. It matters because it affects how the world views the issue. Even when the names we use are inaccurate, they do name something and can give people the cultural space to talk about their lives.

Sociologist Tey Meadow has found that both trans children and, especially, those parents supportive of their trans kids have become highly adept at using and remixing the ideas of medicine, psychology, religion, and secular spirituality. They use this remix to explain who their children are and why they need and deserve the support and care of medical professionals, schools, and churches.[2]

No labels can adequately describe the overwhelming variety of sexual expression or gender play in children. How much room do we, as a society, give children to imagine and experiment with all the possible ways they could be in the world and still be—still become—themselves? Young children's play-acting is a form of socialization, as they imagine themselves into the adult roles they will eventually be asked to assume. But this play-acting also has endless, unimagined possibilities. Children may play-act being cowboys or Dallas Cowboys cheerleaders. They may play doctor with one another or interact with their beloved pets in the pretend role of veterinarian, or as if they, too, are a collie or a kitten. All children play and experiment with gender and sexuality in various ways that defy expectations and categories.

The phrase "feeling different" has become an acceptable way to describe the nonconforming child to a heterosexual mainstream culture because it does not explicitly name same-sex desire and behavior. Perhaps people are also comfortable with this phrase because at some point in our lives, every one of us feels different. Watch children play with a doll or stuffed toy, and you can quickly see how ready they are to bend the social rules they are simultaneously learning. What adults may interpret and judge as rebelliousness or immaturity, children may experience as a queer kind of freedom, a divergence from the straight-and-narrow. It may even be that there is no such thing as a straight child at all—if we understand straight not to mean "heterosexual," but regimented and normalized to become heterosexual. Gay and trans may thus describe all children's inventiveness, resilience, and agency, as well as their need for unconditional support from the adults in their lives so that all of these vital potentials can bloom.

PART 5

STRUGGLING IN THE WORLD

POSITIVE VISIBILITY IN THE MEDIA INCREASES TOLERANCE AND ACCEPTANCE OF LGBT PEOPLE

Gay people have always had a "visibility problem." Since the formation of the first gay rights groups in the 1950s, and increasingly so since the Stonewall riots in 1969, the LGBT movement has been deeply concerned about the visibility of lesbian and gay people and their issues in the media. This concern, in addition to the simple factual accuracy of news stories, has often centered on whether the images that did appear in the media were what they termed positive. They believe, along with many straight people, that positive visibility is connected to tolerance and acceptance of LGBT people.

The problem is that all images, positive or negative, are seen as such only according to how they reflect the larger culture's values. Negative images are negative because they reflect ideas disapproved by mainstream culture. Positive images are positive because they reflect what the mainstream culture already approves. As a result, positive images may increase tolerance and a conditional acceptance, but only within the terms already set by mainstream culture and its values. For the LGBT movement to garner a broader form of acceptance—one that makes room for individual difference and creates conditions that can change what is harmful about society—will entail the creation of images that reflect new values.

To understand the relationship among contemporary images, cultural values, and social change, we need to know some history. For many centuries, same-sex behaviors (as well as a wide range of nonreproductive heterosexual behaviors) were frequently believed to be so terrible that they could cause entire civilizations to tumble. Early European lawmakers based their legal codes on interpretations of Christian law that severely punished homosexual acts (see myth 10, "All Religions Condemn Homosexuality"). Frequently, lawmakers, refusing to even name it, would refer to homosexual behavior as "the unmentionable vice" and "the unspeakable crime against nature." Such language had the paradoxical effect of emphasizing the enormity of the crime's importance by ostensibly silencing its name. This is equivalent to the command, in the Harry Potter series, never to speak Lord Voldemort's name aloud; calling him "He-Who-Must-Not-Be-Named" actually made him more mysterious and powerful. One of the first medical studies of homosexuality, Richard von Krafft-Ebing's *Psychopathia Sexualis, with Especial Reference to Contrary Sexual Instinct: A Medico-Legal Study* (1887), alternated between Krafft-Ebing's native German and Latin. Krafft-Ebing reverted to Latin when he was writing directly about same-sex desire and acts. This reinforced the idea that homosexuality was something not to be mentioned in ordinary speech. Historically, the problem of visibility has been to find a way to speak about homosexuality by clearly naming it without the mystery and threat surrounding it that were generated by these religious and legal condemnations.

In the 1950s, during the early years of the gay rights movement, while activists struggled to correct grossly wrong misperceptions of homosexuals in the media, they were deeply ambivalent about being too visible. At a time when you could be arrested for simply being "too gay" walking down a street or fired if your boss suspected you were gay (which is still the case in many states today), invisibility was a survival tactic. By the late 1960s—thanks to the changes brought about by the civil rights movement, the radical black power movement, feminism, and the sexual revolution—America was a more liberal society. Embracing and publicly claiming your identity were a positive goal. Naming who you were was becoming safer as well.

This change could be seen in media coverage. A good example is two feature pieces on homosexuality published less than a decade apart in the very popular, heavily illustrated magazine *Life*, which appeared weekly on the coffee table of almost every home in America. In the June 26, 1964, issue of the magazine, the article "Homosexuality in America" is filled with such sentences as "[Homosexuals] are part of what they call the 'gay world' which is actually a sad and often sordid world." The images that ran with the article were of men in dimly lit bars or standing alone on street corners. Moderately evenhanded (the author states that only a small minority of gay men are interested in young boys), the article is less sympathetic than pitying. Five years later, although society was still very homophobic, the message of the newly formed, radical gay liberation movement was "come out" and be visible. Gay and lesbian visibility was now a clearly articulated political concern. After the 1969 Stonewall riots, lesbian and gay media watch groups sprung up across the country to hold newspapers, magazines, and television stations responsible for their coverage. The December 31, 1971, issue of *Life* ran a feature article titled "Homosexuals in Revolt," which is largely sympathetic and filled with images of gay protest marches, gay country communes, men in drag, and lesbian activists. The word *gay* is no longer in quotes, and the piece approvingly cites activist Frank Kameny explaining, "The homosexual proved that he could fight back and believe me, until we get what we want we are going to keep on shoving back."

Comparing these two *Life* articles demonstrates how radical social change is reflected in the media. Society was changing, and LGBT people were less stigmatized in the media. But this was not caused by a more accepting media. It was LGBT people who demanded acceptance, demanded change, and demanded to be treated with respect. The shift in representation was first and foremost a political shift. LGBT activism caused the media to change their attitudes and their reporting.

There is no question that there are still many negative images of gay men, lesbians, bisexuals, and transgender people in the media. Newspapers, magazines, television shows, movies, books, blogs, sermons, political campaigns, and even some school textbooks present homosexuals, whether out of ignorance or ill intentions, as sinful, mentally unbalanced, diseased, pathetic, a danger to children, and even psychopathic. These images do harm, and combating them is a political necessity. How should we respond to them?

In the 1970s, when many cities were hosting their first gay pride parades, there was considerable opposition expressed by many members of the gay and lesbian community to the presence of drag queens in their flamboyant outfits because they gave a "bad image" of the community. Similar opposition was leveled against women and men in the leather community. This self-censoring impulse was aimed at films, as well. In 1972, New York's Gay Activist Alliance picketed the New York Film Festival for screening openly gay German director Rainer Werner Fassbinder's film *The Bitter Tears of Petra von Kant*, about unhappy lesbian relationships. In 1976, they repeated the picket for the director's *Fox and His Friends*, about an upper-class gay man exploiting his working-class lover. Gay activists also picketed such films as *The Boys in the Band* (1970), *Cruising* (1980), and *Basic Instinct* (1992) for their "negative" images of LGBT life and people. Ironically, all of these films have since become staples of queer studies courses in colleges and universities.

In 1985, New York activists, including Jewelle Gomez and Vito Russo, formed the social action group Gay and Lesbian Alliance Against Defamation (GLAAD) to protest the inflammatory and medically inaccurate AIDS coverage in New York City newspapers. Under pressure, the papers began reporting more accurately.[1] In 1987, GLAAD persuaded the *New York Times*, which up to that point still insisted on using the term "homosexual" rather than "gay," to change its editorial policy. Eventually GLAAD, and many of the other post-Stonewall media watch groups, expanded their mission to protest not only gross distortions and outright lies about LGBT life, but to praise media outlets that provided "positive" images of gay people. These are two very different approaches to visibility. In the first example, GLAAD forthrightly, unashamedly, and accurately confronts lies told about LGBT people; its response to media distortions was not aimed at making LGBT people less scary or more likable to mainstream society. But when groups began to insist that media outlets replace negative images with positive ones, it was for the explicit purpose of making homosexuals less scary, and more acceptable—just like everyone else. What began as a much-needed battle to confront unjust and degrading images and false information often became essentially a public relations campaign to promote LGBT people and life in glowing and sympathetic terms. The LGBT movement was not the only political movement to take this path of promoting positive images. The feminist and civil rights movements, after protesting the media's misguided and distorted images of women and African Americans, also often called for "positive" images.

There are very real differences between—and different implications for—combating and correcting blatantly, intentionally wrong information, and purposely creating and promoting texts or images that portray gay people as "normal" or regular. Advocating for often-untrue or superficial positive images is not only ill informed, but fosters a shallow level of discussion and reaffirms mainstream values. That is often the quickest and easiest way to get mainstream culture to accept LGBT people. Campaigns to create positive images of gay and lesbian people essentially rely on an advertising mentality. They rebrand LGBT people in an attempt to sway popular opinion. Think about all of the money the makers of Coke spend to tell you that Coke is better than Pepsi, and all of the money the makers of Pepsi spend for you to believe the opposite. Advertising is a business in which producers of products use money and slick sales slogans to increase their market share. The hopes, dreams, emotions, desires, and lives of LGBT people are not reducible to one neat story line, nor are they a product to be packaged and sold to foster a political brand loyalty.

Advertisers frequently use sex to sell products. Sexual (and romantic) images fuel our movies, television shows, and music. From popular print venues such as *People* and *Seventeen* to more serious news programming on network television, much of American media is obsessed with sex. This is even more so where the topic of homosexuality is concerned. Expectations about, concerns over, fear of, and attraction to issues of gay male and lesbian life permeate our media. For example, look at the many news stories about antigay discrimination, the speculation as to which Hollywood stars might be lesbian or gay, and the presence of same-sex marriage announcements in many local and national newspapers.

These are largely manifestations of a fascination and a curiosity that focus only on the surface. Despite the media's interest in sex and sexual behavior in general and homosexuality in particular, there is very little substantive discussion of sexuality. As a culture, Americans are simultaneously obsessed with sex and unable or afraid to really talk, or think deeply, about it. In-depth discussions about the complexities of sexual life and desire are difficult, in part, because they would require not having pat answers. In recent years, some LGBT groups have complained about the use of the word "fag" on *South Park* and the violent imagery in Eminem's lyrics. Is the problem hurtful words per se or the fact that there is inadequate cultural space, in schools or around the dinner table, to dig deep, discuss, and debate what these words mean and where they come from? In forty years, will these shows and songs, like *The Bitter Tears of Petra von Kant* and *The Boys in the Band*, have become iconic artifacts of LGBT culture? American media and public life have a larger problem than gay visibility. We have not developed a language to publicly discuss and ask truly open-ended questions about sex, desire, and the endless emotional dimensions of sexuality for everyone.

Political and social action needs to lead the media, not the other way around, to expand our language. But this action can produce new, more truthful, and more realistic images only if it makes room for the messiness of reality. The reason activists battled to correct false and homophobic information and images in the media was to present what they believed to be the truth to the American public. But the truth is not about positive images. Positive images often actually conspire with mainstream culture's desire not to change. They are a false measure of social progress. It eventually became evident that the strength of lesbian and gay pride marches came from celebrating the incredible diversity of the entire community—and worrying less about presenting a positive image of which some mythical lesbian and gay "we" could all be proud. True equality values difference; it should not demand sameness. Equality emerges out of accurate, endlessly varied, and complex depictions of LGBT people and their lives. Novelist Dodie Bellamy once stated, in response to feminists claiming that they wanted more positive images of women, that she herself was far less interested in positive images of women than in complex and compelling ones. Can we expect, and hope for, the same from LGBT images?

Visibility and positive images—particularly in representational art such as film, novels, theater, and television—is, at heart, a false issue. Today, LGBT people are visible in many ways we have never seen before. The problem LGBT people face is to actually be "public"—that is, fully present and able to partake of the totality of citizenship and life in our American social and political worlds. Fighting for these legal rights and social possibilities is far more important than worrying about how they are viewed by others through "positive images." The longing for positive images is an expression of a wish for things to be different, to be better. If we insist on speaking the complicated truths, and countering lies, about LGBT people, we can make a positive change in how media represent LGBT people and their lives, and change society along with it.

MYTH 18

COMING OUT TODAY IS EASIER THAN EVER BEFORE

In 2012, popular media venues such as the *New York Times*, *Huffington Post*, and *Entertainment Weekly* all suggested in feature articles that being gay is not a big deal anymore. The articles argued this was so manifestly true that gay celebrities no longer even needed to come out. As opposed to past years, when celebrities such as Ellen DeGeneres came out with a big splash, Anderson Cooper was praised for doing so in a new, more casual way. Similarly, other celebrities, including Wanda Sykes, Chris Colfer, Zachary Quinto, and Frank Ocean, have not turned coming out into a major PR campaign. These celebrities want to be out without having to come out. That's the new normal. But does that mean that it is easier to come out today than ever before?

Mainstream media continually interpret the rise of out LGB public figures to mean that coming out and being LGB is no big deal. The message is that lesbian, gay, and bisexual lives finally fit in with a mainstream, majority culture, and that straight people are now more accepting of gay people. None of the celebrities mentioned above appears to have been professionally punished for coming out. This is a good thing. Nevertheless, their experience is hardly typical of all LGB people.

The most important thing to realize about the coming-out process is that people always come out from the closet. Even if they do so casually, there is no neutral starting place for the formation of a public gay identity. Coming out is easier or more difficult for one person versus another because of an individual's circumstances—including such variables as class, race, region, and religion. Crucially, coming out can also be easier or more difficult for the same person depending on circumstances at a given moment. For example, is she with people she knows and trusts, or dependent on strangers, as someone might be at a hospital emergency room? The variability and uncertainty about how any coming-out scene is going to go are inherent to what it means to be in, or out, of the closet, no matter the circumstances. In an April 24, 1990, letter to the *Village Voice*, lesbian novelist Sarah Schulman wrote, "Having to hide the way you live because of fear of punishment isn't a 'right,' nor is it 'privacy.' Being in the closet . . . is maintained by force, not choice."

One function of the closet is to maintain the status quo. This is also why it can be so difficult to come out. To come out is to risk upsetting this precarious balance of what is and is not acceptable, of what people know and don't know about you. This balancing act may never end. Once you are out, people may still interpret everything you say and do through a host of stereotypes, both negative and positive, about what it means to be gay. You are out of the closet, but there is now a new status quo. The pressures that keep people in the closet also determine what it means to be gay outside of the closet. The challenge is how to manage this new reality. For celebrities seeking to preserve their professional careers, this may mean not making a big deal about coming out or their sexuality. Coming out as transgender involves different risks and complications (see myth 3, "All Transgender People Have Sex-Reassignment Surgery").

Paradoxically, the belief that out gay celebrities are positive role models and examples for how things can and do get better only grows stronger the more difficult coming out is for everyone else. This is especially true for LGB people who live at the economic margins, disproportionately young queers of color. Amber Hollibaugh, co–executive director of the activist organization Queers for Economic Justice, says, "If you come out now and you come from poverty and you come from racism, [or] you come from the terror of . . . immigrant communities or communities where you're already a moving target because of who you are, this is not a place where it's any easier to be LGBT even if there's a community center in every single borough."[1] The lifesaving costs of hiding sometimes outweigh the life-threatening costs of coming out.

Racial, economically oppressed, and gender identities compound the difficulty of coming out, because they also require careful decisions about disclosure and the management of what sociologist Erving Goffman calls "spoiled identity."[2] For example, black children are still told by their mothers not to act "suspiciously" around white people. Women are still told not to dress "provocatively" for their own safety. Something similar is at stake for gay people. For many, coming out does not end the need to manage their reputation or what people know about them, worries about safety, or even the need to keep deciding when or whether to disclose their sexuality—yet again—every time they enter a new situation.

This is especially true when we look at how levels of safety and danger differ across job, school, family, religion, the Internet, and even age. Perhaps a lesbian is out to close friends at work but not to her boss, because of the real fear she could be fired just for being gay (see myth 19, "Antidiscrimination Laws in the United States Protect LGBT People"). Or a young gay man may be more out at school than at home, fearing that his parents might kick him out. These aren't idle fears. About 40 percent of homeless youths in the United States are LGBT. According to "Growing Up LGBT in America," a 2012 Human Rights Campaign (HRC) study of LGBT youth, 61 percent are out at school, 11 percent at work, and 8 percent at church. And while 56 percent are out to their immediate family, only 25 percent are out to their extended family. The promise of "safe spaces," such as classrooms or offices where youths can feel less threatened to identify as LGBT, reflects the reality that, for so many LGBT people, and especially LGBT youths, coming out still means leading a double, or triple, life.

Even gay people who have been out for most of their adult lives and believe there is no one left to tell may find themselves thrown back into the closet due to changed circumstances. For example, lesbian or gay seniors who require short- or long-term residential nursing care may face ignorance or hostile environments. They may be unable to safely disclose their sexual identity without jeopardizing their care. Nursing homes and hospitals may turn into huge late-life closets for LGB people who hoped and believed they were done with all that.

Over the past two decades, the Internet has profoundly shifted the idea and the realities of privacy. This is particularly true for LGB people managing the information other people know about them. For example, some people come out only online. According to the HRC study, "73% of LGBT youth say they are more honest about themselves online than in the real world, compared to 43% among non-LGBT youth." The ease of disclosing your real self online comes with a catch: Internet sex and dating sites involve carefully composed profiles, pictures, and chat. Freely expressing your desire online may involve new forms of information-management in order to promote the most attractive version of your real self.

The reason some people don't come out, or come out only online, is because sexuality is already everyone's business. Our culture tells us that sexual identity is one of the most important things to know about a person. This is why people try to keep information about their sexuality, especially a nonheterosexual identity, from circulating without their knowledge. In her 2012 Golden Globes speech, Jodie Foster made a very big and very public deal about not coming out in order to say that her sexual identity was no big deal because it was a private matter. Asserting a zone of privacy, some area of life others may not properly inquire into, is important for many people, not just for award-winning actresses. But as with the gay or lesbian senior who needs nursing care, not every LGB person is equally positioned to ask for or receive such privacy.

The reality is that we do not always know who else already knows or suspects something about us. This not knowing is exhausting and can make LGB people want to close their closet doors even tighter. But what if we lack the ability to close a literal door behind us? When poor people or, especially, homeless people, don't have access to privacy in the sense of a room of their own with a door they can close, they might not even consider coming out because that information would automatically be public.

Anxieties about what other people may or may not know about homosexuality influenced the first gay and lesbian rights organizing in the United States in the 1950s. During these early years, gay male and lesbian activists believed homosexuals could be integrated into American society only if homosexuality conformed to dominant heterosexual norms. Conformity to mainstream norms meant overcoming what psychiatrists at the time called the "homosexual character" and the angry, rebellious personality driving it. The public attempts and internal struggles of gay men and lesbians to overcome such stereotypes—and soften the stigma associated with being homosexual—are deftly explained by Goffman in his now-classic studies of the management of stigma and the presentation of self in everyday life.

Goffman analyzes the severe rules governing everyday social interaction and successful "impression management." These rules parallel advice provided in contemporary coming-out guides. Goffman's theory is that people determine and assess the factors that will dictate their next "move." They make an informed anticipation of how another person might react, evaluate what is mutually known or not known, and attempt to judge other people's personal attributes and capacities.[3] The need to stick to your part in shared social scripts about sexuality, together with the requirement that others play along, exerts enormous internal pressure on how gay people come out. It is also exhausting to have to anticipate every possible scenario, and to realize that you probably missed a few. Above all, differences in circumstance and situation demonstrate how coming out is never a one-time event. The closet is portable: coming out happens over and over again, sometimes moment by moment.

The dynamics of coming out tell us much about the way everyone negotiates sexual desire. Although people are presumed straight unless proven otherwise, many heterosexuals nonetheless have to engage in all manner of "impression management." They edit out sexual desires, practices, and fantasies that will not be perceived as normal. Sexual reputation matters to heterosexuals, too. Worry over reputations and impressions can also exist between two gay people, especially if one person is more out than the other.

No one, gay or straight, is ever fully "out" with her or his sexuality. What's more, there are many aspects of desire that remain unknown to us all (see myth 1, "You Can Tell Who's Gay Just By Looking"). While straight people don't need to justify themselves as heterosexuals, LGB people constantly have to justify themselves. Some LGB people may find they have even more explaining to do. This is because the media's promotion of particular celebrity models of gay identity—models that take for granted being white, middle-class, focused on marriage and family, and profoundly unthreatening—end up creating a new series of exclusions. Positive role models can potentially become a straightjacket for LGB people when they decrease the room left to be lesbian, gay, or bisexual in many different ways. Acceptance and understanding, let alone meeting the acceptable cultural standard, are not automatic. They are work. Those many gay people who don't fit the new normal have more work to explain why their gay lives are not like Rachel Maddow's or Frank Ocean's.

The coming-out process today has often become a list of obligations to make other people feel comfortable about your homosexuality. These other people may include straight family members and friends, but can also extend beyond them. There are coming-out guides for the family members of gay people, such as Robert Bernstein's *Straight Parents, Gay Children: Keeping Families Together* (2003), to help them manage the work they may have to do when their child comes out. Learning that a child is gay can be difficult for a parent. Parents may find they have to confront their own feelings, often of discomfort, about homosexuality for the first time. Or the parents or family members of a gay son or daughter may find that they are now living in a closet of their own. They are faced with deciding when or whether to "come out" to their friends, their pastor or rabbi, or extended family members about their loved one. This pressure may magnify the burden their son or daughter, brother or sister, is carrying. Gay children frequently do everything and anything to put their parents and family members at ease, making sure that their coming out is not too hard on their family. This reassurance might take the form of saying, "I'm the same person you have always known, I want the same things I have always wanted, I am just like you." This might be true for some young gay people saying these words—but it might not be.

The problem is that there is often not a lot of room for a gay person to come out and tell her parents the full truth about herself, without fear of losing parents' love and support, let alone fear of prompting their anger and violence. For the queer child who cannot go along with the idea that being gay is "just like" being straight, coming out—far from establishing conditions for truth-telling and real intimacy—can actually be a deeply estranging experience.

Coming out did not use to be such a private, almost family affair. The phrase "to come out" was first used among gay men in the 1920s, with the implicit and sometimes explicitly stated promise that you were coming out "into the life": the gay life. Coming out referred to a young gay man's formal presentation at a gay urban drag ball, a parody of a society girl "coming out" at a debutante ball. In the following decades, coming out could also mean your first homosexual experience or participation in a community of same-sex-attracted people, people like you. Coming out was a movement into a new social space, created and inhabited by many other gay people.[4]

Gay liberationists of the late 1960s and early 1970s did not downplay their sexual "rebelliousness" as 1950s gay activists did. They saw coming out as a way to change the world rather than adjust to it. In a famous 1970 manifesto, "Gay Is Good," lesbian activist Martha Shelley wrote, "The function of a homosexual is to make you [heterosexuals] uneasy."[5] This was the beginning of coming-out guides published by both mainstream and independent gay and lesbian presses. These early books celebrated sex and sexual cultures, such as gay male bathhouses, butch/femme roles for lesbians, and gay bars. They promoted the understanding of coming out as publicly claiming a homosexual identity.

This history is important because it helps us see that the question of whether you come out is really the question of what kind of gay person you want to be. The desire to change the world and the willingness to make heterosexuals uncomfortable are very far from what it means to come out today.

Many same-sex-attracted teenagers have dropped using labels such as gay and lesbian in order to define themselves against the haunting stereotypes of the militant, in-your-face liberationist gay.[6] These teenagers are not disavowing their attractions but distancing themselves from labels with a stigmatized history for purposes of social acceptance by their straight peers. The *Advocate* explored this trend in two uncritical articles: "Same-sex but Not 'Gay'" (2005) and "Is Gay Over?" (2006). These stories help prop up the myth that coming out is easier today than ever before.

Coming out is a social event. It is inseparable from a longer history of stereotypes about what being gay means. In the late 1980s, the image of the gay man dying of AIDS became one of the most potent visual markers of what it meant to be gay. Since then, all LGB people have been forced to confront this stereotype and its many meanings. In the 1990s, coming-out guides minimized the sex they once celebrated because of the alleged rise of its dangers. Book after book warned that after you come out, you must reassess the very terms of family, relationships, spirituality, love, work, and community. To come out was to mature, grow up, and move away from a historically stigmatized and threatening gay group identity. This maturation often also meant a movement from the public life of bars into the privacy of nuclear families, albeit same-sex ones.

The myth about how easy it is to come out today is the result of an unavoidable bargain (see myth 17, "Positive Visibility in the Media Increases Tolerance and Acceptance of LGBT People"). You can come out as gay as long as your gay identity fits into the straight world. But what of the difficulty in maintaining the impression that you are just like a gay celebrity role model? Or just a "good" LGB person, who wants what every mature person is supposed to want? And what of those many LGBT people who might not make a good first or second impression? Far from being easy, coming out into this compromised world still brings endless work for everyone.

ANTIDISCRIMINATION LAWS IN THE UNITED STATES PROTECT LGBT PEOPLE

In twenty-nine US states—a majority of the country—it is perfectly legal to fire someone just because she or he is lesbian, gay, or bisexual. The situation is even worse for transgender people. Only sixteen states provide legal workplace protections on the basis of both sexual orientation and gender identity. Five other states have laws forbidding discrimination on the basis of sexual orientation, but not gender identity, in employment, housing, and public accommodations.[1] The bottom line: in thirty-four states, transgender people can lose their jobs, or never even be considered for a particular job, simply because of their gender identity or gender expression.

Workplace protections, when offered, cover a variety of discrimination: being harassed or intimidated by co-workers; being demoted or denied a promotion; being fired outright. Civil remedies vary from state to state but typically mandate that the employee first pursue an internal appeals process at the workplace. If no resolution is reached, the employee can file a complaint with state authorities. This may allow her to seek reinstatement, back pay, or restoration to membership in a union. Some states can levy penalties or fines against employers who have violated antidiscrimination statutes.

A few governors have issued executive orders offering some

limited workplace protections to LGBT people. However, administrative policies are not permanent and can be revoked by a governor's successor. This happened in Louisiana, in 2008, when in-coming Republican governor Bobby Jindal rescinded preceding Democratic governor Kathleen Babineaux Blanco's executive order barring workplace discrimination against lesbian and gay state employees. Moreover, administrative policies do not have the same force as law. In the ten states where governors have used executive authority to add workplace protections for LGBT people, workers who believe they have been discriminated against can file a complaint with human resources at their company or agency. They cannot seek legal remedy, nor are employers in these states subject to civil penalties for violating the administrative order—which they would be under an antidiscrimination law.

These may seem like fine-grained distinctions, but the differences matter. LGBT people should be able to go about their lives with equal hopes, security, and opportunities as heterosexuals. Antidiscrimination law puts teeth into the evolving social norm that it is wrong, as a matter of basic fairness, to discriminate on the basis of sexual orientation and gender identity. In numerous national surveys, a clear majority of Americans have said they believe discrimination against LGBT people is wrong. Even people who say they are personally opposed to homosexuality or same-sex marriage support antidiscrimination laws.[2] This support cuts across demographics of religion, generation, and race, finding majority approval among Catholics, senior citizens, and African American churchgoers. Americans, it seems, by a large majority, believe in the fair and equal treatment of LGBT people.

This may all sound very positive, but the situation is more complex. Many Americans also believe that LGBT people are already protected by existing antidiscrimination laws. They are surprised to find out that someone can be fired just for being gay (or appearing to be gay) or for being transgender or gender nonconforming. An unexpected finding in a 2011 survey of likely voters' attitudes about workplace antidiscrimination protections noted that, while 73 percent supported such protections, almost 90 percent mistakenly believed federal law already protected LGBT people. Pollster Jeff Krehely writes, "These numbers show the huge disconnect between voter perceptions about workplace protections and the realities that gay and transgender people face on the job."[3] This disconnect has grave consequences. Not only does it mean that—despite many Americans believing in a basic precept of equality—LGBT people are, largely, not protected in the workplace. More important, it gives conservatives a pretext for arguing that civil equality for LGBT people—especially when enacted through antidiscrimination laws—is really a form of "special rights" or "special protections" (see myth 11, "Gay Rights Infringe on Religious Liberty"). If many Americans believe LGBT people are already protected from workplace discrimination then, clearly, LGBT people are asking for more than what every other American has.

The idea that LGBT people are demanding more than their fair share leads to outlandish assertions by conservatives. In 1993, former attorney general Edwin Meese appeared in an antigay video, *Gay Rights, Special Rights*, produced by the Traditional Values Coalition. In an attempt to reframe antidiscrimination laws as an encroachment on the civil rights of the general public, Meese dramatically stated, "As a white male I have no rights whatsoever, other than what is shared with everyone else."[4] Meese's statement, in addition to its internal incoherence—in fact, he has all the rights everyone has, thus negating the argument that he has none as a white man—is a prime example of how conservative rhetoric uses emotion and a skewed sense of fairness to attack basic protections for LGBT people.

Civil rights are indeed what everyone has simply by being an American. In reality, though, many groups—people of color, women, religious minorities, the disabled—face discrimination in housing, job opportunities, and access to public accommodations. They are often also violently harassed and intimidated when they attempt to exercise basic rights of citizenship, such as voting. African Americans have faced this illegal harassment ever since African American men were granted the vote in 1870. This harassment continues today. Civil rights laws—such as the landmark Civil Rights Act of 1964, which forbids discrimination on the basis of race, color, religion, sex, or national origin, and the Americans with Disabilities Act of 1990—extend to disenfranchised groups the basic civil rights they should have had all along.

Civil rights protections are not special rights. They are laws and policies enacted to ensure that individuals are not denied, just because of who they are, fair and equal access to employment, housing, public accommodations, voting, jury service, and lines of credit. These civil rights laws have not ended discrimination; they have provided enforceable legal remedies when discrimination does occur.

As vital as they are, civil rights laws do not necessarily resolve discrimination and maltreatment. Many Americans would probably agree that people should not be harassed or intimidated on the basis of any of their identities. But they might disagree, profoundly, about when an off-color "joke," or how many off-color jokes, about gay men or about women become intimidation and, thus, illegal. People in historically marginalized groups have been told for years, "It's just a joke. It doesn't mean anything. Get over it." The reality is that these insults, often part of a larger cultural pattern of demeaning words and actions, are intricately connected to a longer history of discrimination and violence. People of color, LGBT people, women, Jews, Muslims, and other minorities are not being overly sensitive or humorless when they do not laugh at jokes told about them. Such jokes are part of a broad, ever-present context of overt threats, physical intimidation, violence, and denial of rights.

Clearly, not every racist, sexist, homophobic, or transphobic joke should be the basis of a lawsuit. And yet, particular words often resonate beyond the moment they were uttered—during a coffee break at the office, in an open dormitory space at a college—to invoke longer social histories and personal memories of real injury. Civil rights laws are designed to lessen the material injuries that can make a crude joke feel unbearable or threatening to the listener, as when that "joke" carries the implicit threat of a lost job if the hearer doesn't find it funny.

Because antidiscrimination laws protecting LGBT people exist only at the state and local levels—and most states don't have them—protection against discrimination depends on whether you are lucky enough to live in the right place. For every state where LGBT people are protected in the workplace, there is another where they can be denied a lease or refused service at a restaurant. This patchwork of state and local laws leaves far too many LGBT people unprotected. It can also result in dangerous legal predicaments as people move from one state to another. For example, a man legally married to his male partner in Massachusetts could be fired from his job for decorating his office cubicle with photos of his wedding if he moved to a state that does not have an antidiscrimination law. Equal rights should cross state lines with you. The long history of struggle for African American civil rights makes clear that a federal law is necessary to supplement state laws where they do exist—and put protections in place where they do not.

For LGBT people, a national remedy would be the proposed Employment Non-Discrimination Act (ENDA). This federal legislation would give LGBT people workplace protections in both public and private employment as long as a company has at least fifteen employees and is not a religious organization. The exclusion of religious organizations is part of the larger history of granting "religious exemptions" to churches and religiously affiliated organizations who object to a state or federal law on religious grounds (see myth 11, "Gay Rights Infringe on Religious Liberty").

But what does it mean for concepts of fairness and equality that a law designed to end discrimination simultaneously allows some groups to discriminate on the grounds of religion—and then only against LGBT people? While religious organizations are no longer legally allowed to discriminate on the basis of race, they are granted considerable leeway to discriminate on the basis of sex and even more to do so on the basis of sexual orientation and gender identity.

If someone who objects, on religious grounds, to renting an

apartment to a gay couple is forced to do so, is the landlord now the victim of discrimination? After all, religion is also protected under the 1964 Civil Rights Act.

A growing number of Christians—evangelicals, but some Catholics, as well—assert that they are the most persecuted group in America.[5] This is an extraordinary assertion, given that Christians are by far the religious majority in the United States. Individuals and organizations making this claim have a long list of complaints that include judicial decisions banning prayer in public schools and the legalization of abortion and "homosexual sodomy." Not surprisingly, the primary alleged perpetrators of these injuries are feminists, homosexuals, secularists, and the activist judges who take their sides in court.[6] To many Americans, this argument about persecuted Christians sounds self-serving. But the people who make them really do feel aggrieved. What can these sentiments tell us about discrimination at the "gut level"?

The terms of this dispute show that the line between fair and unfair, just and unjust, equality and discrimination is not as neat and clean as it may first appear. Both Christian conservatives and LGBT people say they experience discrimination. Both groups sincerely believe this to be true. Both groups even produce evidence to prove their claims. Nonetheless, there is a crucial difference here. Christians are neither a minority nor are they persecuted in the United States as a group. LGBT people, on the other hand, are both a minority group and are frequently victims of discrimination because of it.

It is possible that an individual heterosexual, or white person, or Christian can be discriminated against because of sexual orientation, race, or religious belief. And there is recourse under the law to address that discrimination. But antidiscrimination laws are written to protect historically marginalized groups. So why do people in these majority groups feel oppressed? If you belong to a group that has traditionally enjoyed unquestioned social dominance, any expansion of fairness for other groups—such as people of color,

LGBT people, and non-Christians—might feel like a loss when your taken-for-granted social privileges and legal position are suddenly challenged.[7] Recall Meese's complaint: "As a white male I have no rights whatsoever, other than what is shared with everyone else." What he had was the privilege not to have to fight for the rights "everyone else" was already supposed to be sharing. The lack of national antidiscrimination protections for LGBT people shows how far we are from that reality.

A majority of Americans say they support LGBT antidiscrimination laws. Yet, this does not fully explain exactly what they are for or against in the treatment of people different from themselves. Often, people believe that fairness for everybody else is no less and no more than what feels fair for them.

ENDA will not resolve debates over what feels fair to opponents of homosexuality. These debates are worked out in the give-and-take of actual lives as people agree and disagree. ENDA would, however, make fairness the law of the land.

In its earliest incarnation, in 1974, ENDA covered only sexual orientation. Because of the persistence of trans activists and a struggle within the LGB movement to become inclusive, since 2009, the language of the legislation has included "gender identity." This was not an easy fight. Achieving a trans-inclusive ENDA required overcoming the hostility of some of its congressional sponsors. Some of these women and men, who had already taken a bold leap to support LGB rights, framed their opposition to the inclusion of trans-identity as "pragmatic." They argued that adding "gender identity" would sink the bill's chances of passage. In 2013, a Senate committee voted by a large bipartisan margin, 15–7, to advance a trans-inclusive ENDA to the Senate floor for a vote. The bill has 53 official cosponsors in the Senate; the House version has 177. Regardless of the outcome of the vote by the full Senate, which will take place later in 2013, the legislation's chances of passage in the Republican-controlled House are negligible at best. Previously, in 2012, the Equal Employment Opportunity Commission interpreted

existing federal law—that portion of the 1964 Civil Rights Act that
bans discrimination on the basis of sex—as also protecting workers
on the basis of gender identity.[8]

In 1998, President Bill Clinton signed an executive order protecting civilian federal workers from discrimination based on sexual
orientation. His action effectively overturned a forty-five-year-old
executive order signed by President Dwight Eisenhower, in 1953,
prohibiting the employment of gay men and lesbians in federal
government. The Civil Services Commission stopped enforcing the
Eisenhower-era policy in 1975, but President Clinton's executive
order made the reversal official, and it remains in force. As with the
executive orders signed by governors, presidential directives can
be overturned by successors and do not allow access to the courts
for redress. Thus far, President Barack Obama has resisted calls
to issue an executive order that would ban sexual orientation and
gender identity discrimination by federal contractors. Such a policy
would affect 20 percent of the US workforce. In January 2009, the
Obama-Biden administration did, however, affirm a commitment
to an equal employment opportunity policy that included both sexual orientation and gender identity. But this was an in-house policy
affecting applicants for jobs in the new administration and did not
reach the level of an executive order.

Meanwhile, congressional supporters of ENDA have promised
to keep trying to make the bill federal law. Even if it passes, it will
provide only workplace protections. LGBT people would still not be
protected at the federal level from discrimination in public accommodations, housing, banking, medical care, and so many other vital
areas of life.

The first statewide antidiscrimination statute protecting lesbians and gay men was passed in Wisconsin, in 1982. More than thirty
years later, LGBT people are still struggling to gain basic equality
under the law.

MYTH 20
HATE CRIME LAWS PREVENT VIOLENCE AGAINST LGBT PEOPLE

The mainstream LGBT movement—including national groups such as the National Gay and Lesbian Task Force and Lambda Legal Defense, as well as many local state advocacy groups—often disagrees within itself on political priorities, policy implementation, and even basic strategies regarding social justice issues. But the one thing that almost all of them agree on is that hate crime laws are good for LGBT people, that they work to deter crime, and that LGBT people are safer because of them. These groups are not out of line with liberal American thinking. The National Association for the Advancement of Colored People and the Jewish Anti-Defamation League (ADL) both support hate crime legislation. To make matters appear even simpler, the groups who are most vehemently against hate crime legislation are highly conservative, often overtly homophobic groups, such as Focus on the Family and Concerned Women of America, who fear that such legislation would impede conservative religious people from voicing their beliefs and upholding what they see as "traditional values." But even with widespread liberal support, the basic question remains: do these laws work? Do they deter violence against LGBT people? Do they in fact make LGBT people safer? And, most important, are they fair and just?

The term "hate crime laws" is commonplace, but people often do

not understand the intent or ramifications of such laws. It is important to understand why they were written in order to understand
what they do and don't do. While hate crime laws proliferated in the
early 1980s, their legal roots are deeper. Throughout US history,
violent, discriminatory acts against certain groups of people were
not taken seriously. One solution was to enact new laws to make sure
the laws already on the books were enforced. In the 1930s, when
the lynching of African Americans was pervasive throughout the
country—3,446 black Americans were lynched between 1882 and
1968, one every ten days—activists lobbied Congress to pass antilynching laws. These would allow the federal government to legally
intercede when states would not. A federal law was never passed.
Only in 1968 did the Civil Rights Act make it a federal crime to
"by force or by threat of force, injure, intimidate, or interfere with
anyone . . . by reason of their race, color, religion, or national origin." Soon states began passing their own legislation, based, to a
large degree, on a model drafted by the ADL, to which "gender" and
"sexual orientation" were later added.

Although all of these laws are worded differently, they usually
contain three similar provisions. First, animus against the victim
must be explicitly articulated. That is, the perpetrator must actively
indicate that the crime is being committed because of a "hate" for
the victim's race, religion, ethnicity, or sexual orientation. Second,
state or federal authorities will officially keep track of the number
of incidents by recording them as hate crimes. Third, hate crimes
carry with them "penalty enhancement," usually meaning stiffer
sentencing, because they are understood as injuring not only an individual, but a community. In the New York State penal code, for
instance, if you are convicted of assault in the second degree, a D
felony, you could be sentenced to up to seven years in prison. If
your second-degree assault is recorded as a hate crime, the pros-
ecutor can bump the charge up to a third-degree assault, a C felony,
which carries a sentence of up to fifteen years.

Liberals' support for hate crime laws is not universal, however.
There are progressive LGBT groups, such as Queers for Economic

Justice and the Sylvia Rivera Law Project, that do not support them. There are two main reasons for this opposition. The first is that the laws are disproportionately used against poor people and people of color. The second is that they simply try to fix the problem of bias crime by putting people in prison for longer periods of time, which usually leads to more-hardened criminals. The American Civil Liberties Union (ACLU) has long objected to many hate crime laws because they are predicated on punishing not only action, such as assault, but on punishing constitutionally protected free speech. The ACLU is concerned that hate crime laws criminalize thoughts, arguing that it should not be a crime to think or articulate hurtful statements. Hurting someone's feelings may be offensive, even emotionally painful, but it shouldn't be against the law.

The many religious and conservative groups against hate crime laws, particularly the inclusion of LGBT people as a protected class under the law, fear that they will not only impede but criminalize the articulation of deeply held moral or religious beliefs. Mike Pence, governor of Indiana, lobbied against the federal Matthew Shepard and James Byrd Jr. Hate Crimes Prevention Act when he was a Congressman, stating:

> The issue of hate crimes legislation that continues to be advanced on Capitol Hill is part of a larger effort that we already see working in state statutes. And however well intentioned, hate crimes statutes around the country have been used to quell religious expression. Individual pastors who may wish to preach out of Romans chapter 1 about what the Bible teaches about homosexual behavior . . . could be charged or subject to intimidation for simply expressing a biblical moral view on the issue of homosexual behavior.[1]

Pence's warning has nothing to do with how hate crime legislation actually works. His argument, echoed by many conservative religious groups, is a scare tactic intended to make LGBT activists look like dictators punishing people who do not agree with them. These religious organizations are probably more upset that any protections are being put in place for minority groups.

There are two primary arguments made by proponents of hate crime laws. The first is that their enhanced penalties work to deter attacks on minorities. The second is that they are a fair and just way of dealing with criminal activity, especially when it allegedly terrorizes an entire group. Both are, on the face of it, appealing arguments, pure and simple. But as Oscar Wilde noted in *The Importance of Being Earnest*, "The truth is rarely pure and never simple."

Do hate crime laws deter crime? There is a great deal of research on the question of whether the death penalty is a deterrent to murder. Hundreds of studies have tried to demonstrate that it is, and all have been debunked for statistical and methodological reasons. There is no conclusive evidence that the death penalty works as a deterrent. There have been far fewer studies done on hate crime laws as a deterrent, and none has demonstrated that they deter crimes. Hate crime law proponents will often argue that we don't need scientific proof, only common sense. Many Americans simply accept the unproven assumption that these laws act as a deterrent. Wade Henderson, president of the Leadership Conference on Civil and Human Rights, states, "We recognize we cannot outlaw hate. However, laws shape attitudes. And attitudes influence behavior."[2] He is correct. Laws do shape attitudes. But our legal system does not write laws to shape attitudes; it writes them to justly and fairly punish explicit behaviors.

People who commit crimes and are caught usually get punished. Getting rid of hate crime laws would not let convicted criminals go free. The person who commits a second-degree felony in New York State can already go to prison for seven years. Is doubling—or, as the law euphemistically states it, "enhancing"—that prison sentence from seven to fifteen years going to make it more of a deterrent? Most people and groups, although not all, who oppose hate crime legislation do so because of the enhanced penalty provisions; they see no problem with recording crime statistics in a way that gives a snapshot of social attitudes about LGBT people. But the place to change social attitudes, hearts, and minds is not in prisons. It is in schools, in activist organizations, around the dinner table, at houses of worship, and other places where people can talk, disagree, and learn that disagreement may be a useful and even productive means of growth.

If there is no hard evidence that hate crime laws deter crime, and if people who commit these crimes—which may range from intimidation and harassment to assault, vandalism, and arson—are, if caught, often given harsh punishments under existing law, why do LGBT people, and others, feel so deeply about the need to have them? One of the most prominent hate crimes in US history may provide some insight. In 1998, twenty-one-year-old college student Matthew Shepard was found abandoned and brutally beaten in a desolate field in Laramie, Wyoming. He died six days later. Russell Henderson and Aaron McKinney, also both twenty-one, were arrested for his murder. They confessed and were convicted in two separate trials, in 1999 and 2001, and not under a hate crime law, since Wyoming did not have one. They are each serving two consecutive life terms in the Wyoming State Penitentiary. In 2009, the Matthew Shepard and James Byrd, Jr. Hate Crimes Prevention Act was passed, after a decade of obstruction by a Republican Congress, and signed into law by Barack Obama. (James Byrd was an African American man murdered by three white men, two of whom were white supremacists, in Jasper, Texas, in 1998.) The legislation expanded the 1969 federal hate crime law to include religion, national origin, gender, sexual orientation, gender identity, and disability.

In addition to the question of whether Shepard's murder fit the criteria mandated by hate crime laws—was it, as some news reports suggested, a robbery gone horribly wrong with no clearly articulated animus toward homosexuality?—the crime is a case study in how multiple causes can affect people's actions. In "A Boys Life: For Matthew Shepard's Killers, What Does it Take to Be a Man?," in the September 1999 issue of *Harper's*, JoAnn Wypijewski persuasively argues that Shepard's murder had as much, if not more, to do with poverty, economic conditions, a deadly methamphetamine drug culture, and American ideas about masculinity than it did antigay bias.[3] We will never know for certain if Shepard was murdered because he was gay. But we do know that both of his killers were given two consecutive life sentences without possibility of parole without a hate crime law on the books. Even if there had been a state or federal hate crime law in place, it is also highly likely it would not have prevented the murder.

The public outcry engendered by the Matthew Shepard case to include LGBT people as protected categories in existing hate crime laws was not based on criminology or logic, but emotion. Virulent homophobia in our culture often erupts into violence, and LGBT people are truly not safe from it. Rates of violent crimes against transgender people have been sharply rising for years. Hate crime laws make people feel safe and make them feel that the legal system and law enforcement care about them. But "feeling safe" and "being safe" are very different.

There is another, very understandable, reason why people support hate crime laws. That is the basic human emotion of vengeance. LGBT people, as well as many other groups, are well aware of the injustices committed against them. They are also acutely aware of the long history of these injustices in relation to other oppressed groups, such as the appalling and shameful refusal of Congress to pass antilynching laws. The impulse to vengeance is completely understandable. But laws exist precisely to make sure that fairness and justice take the place of vengeance. Just as basing laws on "feeling safe" makes bad legal policy, laws that do not promote fairness and justice have no place in our legal codes.

Does more punishment equal more justice? How and where do we draw the line? What's more, whose hateful behavior rises to the threshold of a hate crime? And whose is cast as a private affair? The truth is, in America, we enforce hate crime laws very selectively. Do parents of LGBT youth who intimidate, harass, and even physically abuse their children because they are queer get charged with hate crimes? How often are the police convicted of hate crimes when they routinely harass, intimidate, or physically abuse LGBT people or people of color? Unless laws can be written and enforced equally and with complete fairness, they are not just.

The issue of unequal enforcement is also the issue of how we conceptualize hate crimes. Is the rape of women by men a hate crime? Some feminists have argued that it is, because heterosexual rape involves the targeting of a woman by a man precisely because of her gender. If rape is a hate crime, why are hate crime laws and penalty enhancements rarely invoked in rape prosecutions? Could the reason be that only men, and a great many men, would be convicted? Hate crimes are imagined by many people to be perpetrated by a small, deviant minority of people, sick criminals, against an equally small minority of outsiders, such as LGBT people or people of color. Naming rape as a hate crime would acknowledge that a majority of the population, women, is at risk and another large segment, heterosexual men, may be responsible.

Kay Whitlock, in her groundbreaking essay "Reconsidering Hate: Policy and Politics at the Intersection," argues that the simple framework of "hate" to describe and punish violence is completely inadequate to address the deeper divisions and schisms in our culture that are the root of the problem. Arresting people, often young people, and placing them, for long periods of time, in prisons that make no attempt at rehabilitation and will undoubtedly subject them to the endemic violence of prisons, are part of the problem, not the solution. Whitlock suggests that the only way we, as a country and a political system, can move beyond a culture of violence is to work from the bottom up, not the top down. We need to address violence and hatred on the most basic interpersonal levels and at the level of small communities. Working within communities, schools, neighborhoods, and organizations to examine the racial, economic, and psychological reasons that are often underpinning these crimes will move us beyond the simplistic rhetoric of an ambiguously defined "hate." This may seem utopian, but community-based groups such as INCITE! Women of Color Against Violence and FIERCE, a New York City group comprised of young people of color, are doing this work already. Hate crime laws do none of this.

GETTING TESTED ON A REGULAR BASIS HELPS PREVENT THE SPREAD OF HIV

Many people assume that getting tested for HIV on a regular basis makes common sense and is unquestionably good medicine. The logic behind this assumption is that you may not know if you've contracted HIV. If you don't know, then you can't get treated for it. If you are having unprotected sex during this time, you may also unintentionally infect others. That's a lot of "ifs" when your life, and others', are on the line. But these "ifs" connected to testing need not be so confusing. The only way to prevent the spread of HIV is by wearing a condom during anal or vaginal intercourse. Testing, in and of itself, does not stop the transmission of HIV. How testing came to be understood, falsely, as a preventive sexual practice, verging on a form of wishfully safer sex, tells a broader story about how we've responded to the AIDS epidemic in the United States since its very beginnings. Reading about this myth could save your life.

The first reported cases of what was later called AIDS (acquired immune deficiency syndrome) were diagnosed in openly gay men showing symptoms of fairly rare diseases, such as Kaposi's sarcoma (KS) and Pneumocystis pneumonia (PCP). In 1981, these cases were reported in *Morbidity and Mortality Weekly Report*, a publication of the Centers for Disease Control and Prevention (CDC). Doctors had no idea what was causing the outbreak. They knew only that it was affecting gay men who lived in urban areas. Pathologists first called the combination of symptoms, which they understood to be not a single disease but a syndrome, "gay-related immune deficiency" (GRID). They had no understanding of how transmission occurred but suspected that it was through exchange of bodily fluids, probably during certain sexual acts, possibly even kissing. Within weeks after the first cases were reported, the mainstream media presented gay male sexual activity and, by association, all homosexuality as dangerous. Although it became immediately apparent that women, IV drug users, and hemophiliacs were also showing the same symptoms, these new at-risk groups did not change the media's focus on gay men.

Media coverage shaped the story that gay men, already understood as abnormal and deviant, were to blame for the outbreak. A fear of gay men and gay male sex had long been rampant in the country. Many media stories stated overtly, or implied, that GRID was punishment by nature or God—or both—for the unchecked gay male "lifestyle" that emerged from the sexual and political liberation movements of the 1960s and 1970s. This promoted hysteria and alleviated the fear that the so-called general public could contract the disease.

In 1983, researchers discovered the virus that caused the drastic suppression of the immune system and ensuing symptoms. It was officially named HIV, for human immunodeficiency virus, in 1986. Infection with HIV did not mean you had full-blown AIDS; the diagnosis of AIDS was given only when a patient was diagnosed with severe symptoms of the opportunistic infections associated with AIDS. Nonetheless, the HIV virus was always present, although sometimes at undetectable levels, in an infected person's semen, blood, breast milk, and/or vaginal fluids. It took years for researchers to discover and understand all of this information.

During this time, gay male and lesbian activists and sex educators began thinking about how to have "safe" sex: sex that would prevent the transmission of HIV by preventing semen from coming into contact with porous mucous membranes in the anus or vagina.

These guidelines were later followed by heterosexuals as well. While safe-sex strategies went through repeated transformations as more information about transmission was discovered, they were all based on simple logic. Where sexual transmission was concerned, HIV could spread only through anal and vaginal intercourse. So, wear a condom.

Under most circumstances, HIV is transmitted from the penetrative to the receptive partner. However, recent studies have demonstrated that it is possible for a woman to transmit HIV to a man through vaginal intercourse. This is especially true if the man is uncircumcised, since the underside of the foreskin of the penis, composed of mucus-membrane-like cells, more easily allows the virus to enter the blood stream. Although HIV can be present in vaginal fluids, it is not present in the rectum. The only chance of contracting HIV from an HIV-positive receptive partner during anal sex is if the rectum is bleeding and the penis has a fissure or is uncircumcised. In all cases, the penetrative and receptive partner can prevent the spread of HIV if the penetrative partner wears a condom. There is no evidence that HIV can be contracted through oral sex.

To be clear: testing is important, necessary, and useful. But it has nothing to do with how HIV is spread. We are debunking the myth about the virtues of regular testing to help stop the spread of HIV and to help you from getting it. It makes complete sense for a sexually active person to know his or her HIV status. According to the CDC, almost eighty percent of HIV-positive men ages eighteen to twenty-four in the United States are unaware they are infected. If you are HIV-positive, knowing your status early can expedite life-saving drug therapy. But you don't need to get tested unless you've had unprotected intercourse, feel you have exposed yourself to HIV by sharing needles, or otherwise come into contact with blood through an open sore or cut.

Nonetheless, testing has come to bear the weight of so many questions and anxieties around sex. This is clear in how the logic of testing has changed in response to a social and cultural history that has identified gay male sex as dangerous, and closely associated gay male identity itself with HIV/AIDS. In the early years of the epidemic, it was imperative for a gay man to know his HIV status because he may well have been engaging in unprotected sex during a time when no one knew about HIV or AIDS. There was a general cultural panic about any sex that was not straight sex. But how, then, could gay men be safe? Using a condom made sense. But the idea of "safe" took on increasingly broader and vaguer meanings. Did safe only mean using a condom? Or also dental dams for oral-genital or oral-anal contact? And what about gloves for fisting? Did safe mean not having sex with too many people? Did safe mean not having sex with the wrong kinds of people? Did safe mean being monogamous with one life-long sexual partner? Did safe sex mean no sex? The cultural dictate to be safe didn't ban sex; it gave a series of contradictory rules and recommendations about having sex, all in the context of fear and confusion.

Things have improved less than you'd expect. The most recent CDC risk-reduction literature lists condom use last among other prevention strategies that include "choosing to stop having sex" and "limiting [your] number of sex partners." These recommendations are, respectively, as unrealistic and inaccurate as they were in response to the very first HIV/AIDS cases. To introduce other ways to be safe beyond wearing a condom does not mean you are more safe; it confuses what being safe means and what exactly the danger is that you're protecting yourself against.

Public health officials, as well as family and friends, continually offered the one suggestion that could cut through all the contradictions they themselves exacerbated: "don't risk it." The message was that any one preventive measure might not be enough. Condoms, for example, did not eradicate or kill infected semen; they only collected it in a thin piece of rubber. The fact that HIV could still be present, if nontransmissible, during sexual activity put the safety and danger of sex into constant question. Fear clouded judgment, and people were being told to get tested because everyone was scared of what could happen. This increased the amount of guilt and shame over doing something wrong, as well as the emotional and psychological power of the possibility of danger. The message was: you could always be safer, but you could never be safe enough. All of this has, ironically, perverted the purpose of testing. We now live in a time when people get tested so they are not scared. The myth that regular, and now widespread, testing for HIV will stop the spread of HIV/AIDS, rather than simply inform you of your health status, is based on the understandable need to feel safe. It is very difficult to resist that need when it's often cloaked in the concerned advice to "be careful" and "stay alive." However, feeling safe is not a prevention strategy. In fact, it is useless when it comes to HIV transmission. The mythology of safety gives a reassuring, yet false, sense of security to you and the people who care about you—and it comes with a high cost.

The ambiguities of danger and safety that drive our national discussions about health, sex, and HIV/AIDS are almost always strictly demarcated along lines of right and wrong, good and bad. This is largely because the confusion and fear of ambiguity are most quickly alleviated through generalization. Anthropologist Mary Douglas writes in her classic study *Purity and Danger: An Analysis of Concepts of Pollution and Taboo* that fear serves a social purpose to contain danger and make it less threatening. Douglas explains, "Ideas about separating, purifying, demarcating and punishing transgressions have as their main function to impose system on an inherently untidy experience. It is only by exaggerating the difference between within and without, about and below, male and female, with and against, that a semblance of order is created."[1]

The logic of repeated testing is part of the social and emotional management of sexual danger. Its false sense of security reinforces the larger narrative that outsider groups such as gay men, bisexual males, sex workers, and men on the "down low" (a term first used to describe African American men, and now adopted by men of all races who have sex with men but don't identify as gay) are all too sexual or inappropriately sexual. Thus they are inherently dangerous and pose severe threats to a system of order and health. Gay men are not immune to this thinking. They come to see one another as safe or dangerous according to stereotypes of age, race, class, geography, and religion. Perceptions of safety also vary depending on how respectable a person seems, how reckless an online profile sounds, or, most tellingly, whether or not potential partners advertise when they were last tested and what their results were.

Ironically, maintaining these imaginary cultural separations as strictly as possible ends up being even more dangerous. Assigning danger to some clearly demarcated people, whose differences you believe are absolute, makes people worry less about themselves. This is clear in abstinence-only education. There is no evidence that abstinence-only education stops young people from having sex or even delays the average age at which they start doing so. But there is clear evidence that young people educated to believe abstinence equals safe sex, and a larger sense of safety, are significantly less likely to use birth control, especially condoms, when they do have sex—leading to the transmission of STIs as well as to pregnancy.

A long-term monogamous couple, whether two gay men or a woman and a man, provides another example. This couple probably already knows each other better than people who have anonymous or casual sex. Their familiarity presupposes health and safety and the belief that there would be no need to use condoms. But this feeling of safety does not take into consideration people's past sexual histories or the possibility of undisclosed affairs. The same pattern may be present in serial monogamy, in which a person has a string of serious sexual relationships, but only one at a time. Our culture has perpetuated the myth that it is not the sexual acts you perform but the number of partners you have that places you at risk for HIV/AIDS. This promotes an irrational fear of out-of-control sexuality. In other words, our culture touts monogamy, including serial monogamy, as a way to feel safe.

People want to feel and be safe. And they don't want to be seen as self-destructive and dangerous to others. Often people get tested to demonstrate not only that they're currently negative but that, in an act of magical thinking, their sexual lifestyle is, was, and will be safe and trustworthy. This is why the "community standard" of responsibility for many gay men is to get tested and share their status with their sexual partners. This is a problem when a positive test result invites rejection, or even vilification, if divulged. People understandably lie about their positive status to ward off rejection. Bisexual men may not even want to have this discussion with women, since it may out them as a man who has sex with men. Many sex workers—male and female—are in even more-difficult positions. If they disclose that they are HIV-positive, they might lose their clients, or possibly put themselves in physical danger if a client becomes angry. Yet their potential unwillingness to divulge their status, or even get tested, is somehow seen as imperiling everyone else. Twenty-four states have enacted laws that criminalize HIV-positive people for not disclosing their status either, in some states, before any sexual act, or in others, before unprotected intercourse. And most cities have increased legal sanctions on sex workers, thus making their lives even more dangerous.

For the generation of gay male youth who grew up in the 1990s and after, safety was conflated with self-esteem, self-acceptance, and individuality. This was not just in regards to gay male sex but health and sex education in general. Repeated testing brings acceptance beyond gay male communities. It also signals responsible sexual citizenship within a mainstream heterosexual public. Ironically, the more widespread cultural validation around testing becomes, the more it separates testing from whether you have actually exposed yourself to HIV through sex. The US Preventive Services Task Force now wants to make testing a regular part of a yearly checkup for everyone, gay and straight. Health officials' emphasis on the potential danger of HIV transmission has created a situation in which the average person is encouraged to exert less personal power and agency to define sexual safety for him- or herself. The result has been decreased competence and knowledge about our sexual selves, relations, and judgments.

The implications for continued HIV transmission are cata-strophic. Infection rates among men who have sex with men have remained steady or increased since the early 1990s—even as they have gone down, overall, among heterosexuals and IV drug users. According to data released by the CDC in 2012, the prevalence of HIV in urban areas among men who have sex with men, ages twenty-three to twenty-nine, increased 16 percent from 1994 to 2008. (Prevalence is defined as the number of persons living with HIV at a given time.) The prevalence of HIV among those ages eighteen to twenty-two remained steady over this time at 11 percent. But between 2008 and 2010, new HIV infections among men who have sex with men increased by 12 percent. For those ages thirteen to twenty-four, the increase was 22 percent. In twenty-one major US cities, one in five men who have sex with men is HIV-positive.

Gay men have not forgotten the danger of HIV. These statistics apply to the generation that grew up under the looming presence of safe-sex messages and education. Nonetheless, they may not be sufficiently outraged over the epidemic for two main reasons. First, because of effective drugs, they may not know people who are dying of AIDS. Second, and more insidious, many gay men have internal-ized the imperative to be "safe," in its varieties of vague meanings, and channeled their worry about HIV and the urgency to "be safe, be safe!" into either getting tested themselves or relying on other men to get tested.

For many people, the logic of testing is now: get tested so you know that you're negative and can have unprotected sex, and then repeat. Drug companies have facilitated this logic, and the compul-sion to get tested, by releasing new at-home rapid HIV tests that make it easier to get tested, share your status, and have unprotected sex. If you feel you need to get tested and don't feel comfortable doing so at a clinic or doctor's office, then taking an at-home test makes sense. However, at-home testing kits can also promote un-warranted fears even as they promote a false sense of safety. How much really is there to worry about if you or your partner always wears a condom? And if you don't? Well, at-home tests also routinize testing as if it should become a new kind of foreplay: what you do before you hook up, often to have condomless sex.

And an even more recent example of contradictory suggestions on how to be safe is the release of pre-exposure prophylaxis (PrEP), drugs that can lower the chance of infection, but at rates significantly lower than a condom. Even though the companies who manufacture these drugs advise that they be used with condoms, many men are excited about the safety the drugs promise because they don't want to wear condoms. The talk surrounding PrEP drugs ultimately increases the real danger of HIV transmission by offering yet another way to be safe, yet not completely.

Having sex without a condom may very well feel more exciting, but how a sex act feels is inseparable from how it's valued socially, culturally, psychologically, and emotionally. Young gay men today must negotiate the proscriptions and prescriptions of a history of pleasure and danger. They view this cultural inheritance as an unnecessary burden of extra sexual responsibility. They reject HIV/ AIDS as not their history, and may even distance themselves from older generations of gay men whom they see as more closely associated with it. Even the CDC recommends, in a pamphlet aimed at those ages thirteen to twenty-four, the very population where one in four new HIV infections occurs, "not having sex with an older person who may be more likely to already have HIV." Following these suggestions does not mean you have clarified the sexual danger for yourself, or lessened your anxiety about it. Quite the opposite.

The mythologies of safety around abstinence, monogamy, and avoiding bad sex can actually lead to HIV transmission. This is equally true of the myth that testing prevents the spread of HIV. It can easily lead to its transmission. The actual danger of transmission is less and less clear to people who get tested when they don't need to or don't know if they need to. So the need to use a condom becomes less clear, too. Testing is only a small part of a much larger myth of safety around sex. All sexuality has unknown risks. So does walking down the street. But in putting too much pressure on the possibility of danger, the safety myth has done two things: obscured the only way HIV transmission can be stopped—by wearing a condom—and created a new, ever-more-powerful risk for transmission: feeling too safe.

ACKNOWLEDGMENTS

Many thanks to all of the people at Beacon Press who were instrumental in our writing this book. Gayatri Patnaik, our editor, was a wonderful mixture of encouraging and patient. Rachael Marks was incredibly helpful answering every question we had. Caitlin Meyer, our publicist, was already at work pitching the book before we had even handed in the manuscript. We also owe much thanks to Richard Voos, who helped us through any number of computer problems and crises. Nao Bustamante, José Muñoz, and Tavia Nyong'o also worked some needed magic with Dropbox. Collectively we would like to thank the following colleagues and friends who have helped us—in conversations, e-mails, and arguments—come to the conclusions we did, even when they may not agree with some of them: Jill Casid, Kevin Cathcart, Sue Hyde, Janet Jakobsen, Tom Luxon, Tey Meadow, Juliet Mitchell, Amber Musser, Alex Nemerov, Linda Schlossberg, Ivy Schweitzer, Laura Wexler, Kay Whitlock, and Angela Zito.

NOTES

MYTH 1

1. Allan Berube, *Coming Out Under Fire: The History of Men and Women in World War Two* (New York: Free Press, 1990), 156.
2. Ibid., 147.
3. George Chauncey, *Gay New York: Gender, Urban Culture, and the Making of the Gay Male World, 1890–1940* (New York: Basic Books, 1994).
4. Nancy Hanley, *Body Politics: Power, Sex, and Nonverbal Communication* (Englewood, NJ: Prentice Hall, 1977), 152.

MYTH 2

1. Alfred C. Kinsey et al., *Sexual Behavior in the Human Female* (Philadelphia: W. B. Saunders Company, 1953), 469.
2. Ibid., 472.

MYTH 3

1. Janice G. Raymond, *The Transsexual Empire: The Making of the She-Male* (Boston: Beacon Press, 1979).
2. Tey Meadow, "Child," *Transgender Studies Quarterly* 1, no. 1 (forthcoming).

MYTH 4

1. "Sexual Abuse: A Major Cause of Homosexuality?," H.O.M.E. (Heterosexuals Organized for a Moral Environment) website, http://www.home60515.com.
2. American Psychiatric Association profile, *Born Gay* website, http://borngay.procon.org/.

3. Jeff Johnston, "Childhood Sexual Abuse and Male Homosexuality," *CitizenLink*, June 17, 2010, http://www.citizenlink.com.

4. John Wihbey, "Global Prevalence of Child Sexual Abuse," *Journalist's Resource*, November 15, 2011, http://journalistsresource.org.

5. Anita Bryant and Bob Green, *At Any Cost* (Grand Rapids, MI: Fleming H. Revell, 1978).

MYTH 5

1. Alfred C. Kinsey et al., *Sexual Behavior in the Human Male* (Philadelphia: W. B. Saunders Company, 1948), 168.

2. George Weinberg, *Society and the Healthy Homosexual* (New York: St. Martin's Press, 1972), 78.

3. Netta Weinstein et al., "Parental Autonomy Support and Discrepancies Between Implicit and Explicit Sexual Identities: Dynamics of Self-acceptance and Defense," *Journal of Personality and Social Psychology* 102, no. 4 (April 2012): 815–32.

MYTH 6

1. Eve Kosofsky Sedgwick, "How to Bring Your Kids Up Gay," *Social Text* 29 (1991): 20; K. J. Zucker and R. L. Spitzer, "Was the Gender Identity Disorder of Childhood Diagnosis Introduced into DSM-III as a Backdoor Maneuver to Replace Homosexuality? A Historical Note," *Journal of Sex & Marital Therapy* 31 (2005): 31–42.

2. Zucker and Spitzer; and Jack Drescher, "Queer Diagnoses: Parallels and Contrasts in the History of Homosexuality, Gender Variance, and the Diagnostic and Statistical Manual," *Archives of Sexual Behavior* 39, no. 2 (2010): 427–60.

3. Gilbert Herdt, ed., *Third Sex, Third Gender: Beyond Sexual Dimorphism in Culture and History* (New York: Zone Books, 1993).

MYTH 7

1. Quoted in Alex Witchel, "Life After 'Sex,'" *New York Times Magazine*, January 19, 2012. For video of the speech (March 13, 2010), see "Cynthia Nixon Accepts the Vito Russo Award at the 21st Annual GLAAD Media Award," March 16, 2010, YouTube.com.

2. Summarized in Marcia Malory, "Homosexuality & Choice: Are Gay

People 'Born This Way?'" *Scientific American*, October 19, 2012, http://blogs.scientificamerican.com. For original study, see Simon LeVay, "A Difference in Hypothalamic Structure Between Heterosexual and Homosexual Men," *Science* 253 (1991): 1034–37.

3. Malory, "Homosexuality & Choice."

4. Rebecca Jordan-Young, *Brain Storm: The Flaws in the Science of Sex Differences* (Cambridge, MA: Harvard University Press, 2010), 144.

5. Edward Stein, *The Mismeasure of Desire: The Science, Theory, and Ethics of Sexual Desire* (New York: Oxford University Press, 1999), 148–53.

6. Ibid., 153.

7. Ibid., 148.

8. Malory, "Homosexuality & Choice"; Stein, *The Mismeasure of Desire*, 267–68.

9. Stein, *The Mismeasure of Desire*, 273.

10. Sigmund Freud, *Three Essays on the Theory of Sexuality* (1905), vol. VII of *The Standard Edition of the Complete Psychological Works of Sigmund Freud*, ed. James Strachey (London: Hogarth Press, 1955), 125–243.

11. Irving Bieber et al., *Homosexuality: A Psychoanalytic Study* (Northvale, NJ: Jason Aronson, 1988), 319.

MYTH 8

1. Marcie Gallo, *Different Daughters: A History of the Daughters of Bilitis and the Rise of the Lesbian Rights Movement* (Seattle: Seal Press, 2006).

2. R. Drummond Ayres, "Gay Woman Loses Custody of Her Son to Her Mother," *New York Times*, September 8, 1993.

3. Charles E. Morris III, "Pink Herring & the Fourth Persona: J. Edgar Hoover's Sex Crime Panic," *Quarterly Journal of Speech* 88, no. 2 (May 2002): 228–44.

4. Judith Stacey and Timothy J. Biblarz, "(How) Does the Sexual Orientation of Parents Matter?," *American Sociological Review* 66, no. 2 (April 2001): 159–83.

MYTH 9

1. Reported in William N. Eskridge Jr., "Six Myths That Confuse the Marriage Equality Debate," *Valparaiso University Law Review* 46, no. 1 (Fall 2011): 107.

2. Stanley Kurtz, "The End of Marriage in Scandinavia: The 'Conservative

Case' for Same-Sex Marriage Collapses," *Weekly Standard*, February 2, 2004, http://www.weeklystandard.com.

3. M. V. Lee Badgett, "Prenuptial Jitters: Did Gay Marriage Destroy Heterosexual Marriage in Scandinavia?," Slate.com, May 20, 2004.

4. Nancy Cott, testimony in Perry et al. v. Schwarzenegger, US District Court, Northern District, vol. 1 (January 11, 2010): 208.

5. David K. Li, "Gay or Straight, Guys Reluctant to Say I Do," *New York Post*, July 5, 2011.

MYTH 10

1. Ruth Vanita, "Hinduism and Homosexuality," in *Queer Religion: Homosexuality in Modern Religious History*, vol. 1, eds. Donald L. Boisvert and Jay Emerson Johnson (Santa Barbara, CA: Praeger, 2012), 1–23. See also Arvind Sharma, "Homosexuality and Hinduism," in *Homosexuality and World Religions*, ed. Arlene Swidler (Valley Forge, PA: Trinity Press, 1993), 70.

2. Janet R. Jakobsen and Ann Pellegrini, *Love the Sin: Sexual Regulation and the Limits of Religious Tolerance* (Boston: Beacon Press, 2004). Much of this chapter is indebted to the joint work of Jakobsen and Pellegrini in *Love the Sin* and elsewhere.

3. José Ignazio Cabezón, "Homosexuality and Buddhism," in *Homosexuality and World Religions*, 81–101; Robert Shore-Goss, "Queer Buddhists: Re-Visiting Sexual Gender Fluidity," in *Queer Religion*, 25–49.

4. Bernadette Brooten, *Love Between Women: Early Christian Responses to Female Homoeroticism* (Chicago: University of Chicago Press, 1996).

5. Khalid Duran, "Homosexuality and Islam," in *Homosexuality and World Religions*, 181–82.

6. Aisha Geissinger, "Islam and Discourses of Same-Sex Desire," in *Queer Religion*, 69–90, esp. 74–80.

7. Geissinger, "Islam and Discourses of Same-Sex Desire," 80–84.

8. Daniel Boyarin, "Are There Any Jews in 'The History of Sexuality'?," *Journal of the History of Sexuality* 5, no. 3 (January 1995): 339.

9. Rebecca T. Alpert, "Religious Liberty, Same-Sex Marriage and the Case of Reconstructionist Judaism," in *God Forbid: Religion and Sex in American Public Life*, ed. Kathleen Sands (New York: Oxford University Press, 2000), 124–32.

10. Jakobsen and Pellegrini, *Love the Sin*, 127–47.

MYTH 11

1. Andrew Koppelman, "You Can't Hurry Love: Why Antidiscrimination Protections for Gay People Should Have Religious Exemptions," *Brooklyn Law Review* 72, no. 125 (2006–07): 136.
2. Martha Minow, "Should Religious Groups Be Exempt from Civil Rights Laws?," *Boston College Law Review* 48 (2007): 786.
3. "Enforcement Standards for Licensing Regulations," 102 Mass. Code Regs. 1.03(1) (2007).
4. Jana Singer, "Balancing Away Marriage Equality," *SCOTUSblog*, August 29, 2011, http://www.scotusblog.com.
5. Winnifred Fallers Sullivan, *The Impossibility of Religious Freedom* (Princeton, NJ: Princeton University Press, 2005).
6. Bob Jones University v. United States, 461 US 574 (1983), 605.
7. Minow, "Should Religious Groups Be Exempt from Civil Rights Laws?," 848.

MYTH 12

1. Cheryl Clarke, "The Power to Transform: Homophobia in the Black Community," in Barbara Smith, *Home Girls: A Black Feminist Anthology* (New York: Kitchen Table/Women of Color Press, 1983).
2. Kimberlé W. Crenshaw (1991), "Mapping the Margins: Intersectionality, Identity Politics, and Violence Against Women of Color," *Stanford Law Review* 43, no. 6. (1991): 1241–99.
3. Martha Albertson Fineman, *The Neutered Mother, the Sexual Family and Other Twentieth Century Tragedies* (New York: Routledge, 1995).
4. Kim E. Nielsen, *A Disability History of the United States* (Boston: Beacon Press, 2012).

MYTH 13

1. Cited in Winnie McCroy, "The Myth of Lesbian Bed Death," *Village Voice*, June 22, 2010, http://www.villagevoice.com.
2. Navi Pillay, "The Shocking Reality of Homophobic Rape," UN Human Rights Office website, June 20, 2011, http://www.ohchr.org.
3. Ibid.
4. Adrienne Rich, "Compulsory Heterosexuality and Lesbian Existence," *Signs: Journal of Women in Culture and Society* 5, no, 4 (Summer 1980): 631–60.

5. Lisa Duggan and Nan D. Hunter, *Sex Wars: Sexual Dissent and Political Culture* (New York: Routledge, 1995).

6. Muriel Dimen, "Politically Correct? Politically Incorrect?," in *Pleasure and Danger: Exploring Female Sexuality*, ed. Carole Vance (New York: Routledge/Kegan Paul, 1984), 138–48.

7. All of these women are contributors to the important anthology *Pleasure and Danger*.

8. SAMOIS, eds., *Coming to Power: Writing and Graphics on Lesbian S/M*, 2nd revised and updated ed. (Boston: Alyson Press, 1982).

9. Eve Kosofsky Sedgwick, *Epistemology of the Closet* (Berkeley: University of California Press, 2008), 22.

10. Gayle Rubin, "Thinking Sex: Notes for a Radical Theory of the Politics of Sexuality" (1984), in *The Lesbian and Gay Studies Reader*, eds. Henry Abelove, Michèle Aina Barale, and David M. Halperin (New York: Routledge, 1993), 15.

MYTH 14

1. Natalie Shainess, quoted in "The New Bisexuals," *Time*, May 13, 1974.

MYTH 15

1. Anne Fausto-Sterling, *Sexing the Body: Gender Politics and the Construction of Sexuality* (New York: Basic Books, 2000).

2. Genny Beemyn and Susan Rankin, *The Lives of Transgender People* (New York: Columbia University Press, 2011), 33–34.

3. Ibid., 34.

4. Ibid., 35.

5. Amy L. Stone, *Gay Rights at the Ballot Box* (Minneapolis: University of Minnesota Press, 2012).

MYTH 16

1. Tey Meadow, "Child," *Transgender Studies Quarterly*, 1, no. 1 (2013 [forthcoming]).

2. Tey Meadow, "'Deep Down Where the Music Plays': How Parents Account for Gender Variance," *Sexualities* 14, no. 6 (2011): 725–47.

MYTH 17

1. Michael Schiavi, *Celluloid Activist: The Life and Times of Vito Russo* (Madison, WI: University of Wisconsin Press, 2011).

MYTH 18

1. In Lara Flanders, "An Erotic Politics: What's the Future of the LGBTQ Movement?," *Truthout*, June 26, 2012, http://truth-out.org.
2. Erving Goffman, *Stigma: Notes on the Management of Spoiled Identity* (Upper Saddle River, New Jersey: Prentice-Hall, 1963).
3. Erving Goffman, *The Presentation of Self in Everyday Life* (New York: Doubleday, 1959); Erving Goffman, *Strategic Interaction* (Philadelphia: University of Pennsylvania Press, 1969).
4. George Chauncey, *Gay New York: Gender, Urban Culture, and the Making of the Gay Male World, 1890–1940* (New York: Basic Books, 1994), 7–8.
5. Martha Shelley, "Gay Is Good," reprinted in *A History of Our Time: Readings on Postwar America*, eds. William H. Chafe, Harvard Sitkoff, Beth Bailey (New York: Oxford University Press, 2011), 226.
6. Ritch Savin-Williams, *The New Gay Teenager* (Cambridge, MA: Harvard University Press, 2005).

MYTH 19

1. Jerome Hunt, *A State-by-State Examination of Nondiscrimination Laws and Policies: State Nondiscrimination Policies Fill the Void but Federal Protections Are Still Needed* (Washington, DC: Center for American Progress, June 2012), 1, http://www.americanprogress.org.
2. See, for example, Jeff Krehely, "Polls Show Huge Public Support for Gay and Transgender Workplace Protections," Center for American Progress, June 2, 2011, http://www.americanprogress.org.
3. Ibid.
4. Quoted in Janet R. Jakobsen, *Working Alliances and the Politics of Difference: Diversity and Feminist Ethics* (Bloomington, IN: University of Indiana Press, 1998), 131.
5. Elizabeth A. Castelli, "Persecution Complexes: Identity Politics and the 'War on Christians,'" *differences* 18, no. 3 (Fall 2007): 152–80.
6. Ibid., 156.

NOTES

7. Janet R. Jakobsen and Ann Pellegrini, *Love the Sin: Sexual Regulation and the Limits of Religious Tolerance* (Boston: Beacon Press, 2004), 45–73.

8. "Transgender Employees Now Protected by Anti-Discrimination Law After 'Landmark' EEOC Ruling," *Huffington Post*, April 24, 2012.

MYTH 20

1. Annette Seigel Gross, "Mike Pence's Alignment with The Family Research Council: Siding AGAINST Hate Crimes Legislation," Greater Indianapolis for Change website, n.d., http://indyvanguard.org.

2. Wade Henderson, "Why We Need Bias Laws," *New York Times*, March 7, 2012.

3. JoAnn Wypijewski, "A Boy's Life: For Matthew Shepard's Killers, What Does It Take to Pass as a Man," *Harper's*, September 1999.

MYTH 21

1. Mary Douglas, *Purity and Danger: An Analysis of Concept of Pollution and Taboo* (New York: Routledge, 2000), 3–5.